THE CHURCH OF ENGLAND
AND
HER REFORMATIONS

THE
CHURCH OF ENGLAND
AND
HER REFORMATIONS

BY

WILLIAM HOWARD-FLANDERS
(BARRISTER-AT-LAW)

AUTHOR OF
"KING, PARLIAMENT AND ARMY,"
"A THOUSAND YEARS OF EMPIRE,"
"BALKANIA." ETC.

"The good old times of England, 'ere in her evil days,
From their holy faith and ancient rite her people fell
away,
When her gentleman had hands to give and her
yeomen hearts to feel,
And they raised full many a bedehouse, but never
a Bastile."
—JOHN MASON NEALE.

HEATH CRANTON LIMITED
6 FLEET LANE, LONDON, E.C.4
1932

111605

*Printed in Great Britain for Heath Cranton Limited by
Purnell & Sons, Paulton (Somerset) and London*

AUTHOR'S NOTE

In sketching the History of the Reformation of the Church of England, I would first of all say that Reformation in Church and State are closely allied and often proceed from the same causes. One of these is a growing feeling of national self-consciousness which is generally followed by a revival of learning.

William I refused to hold England as a papal fief, and Langfranc held that the Church of England had never been subject to Rome; and, in consequence of the policy of Boniface VIII (1294), who claimed that God had placed in his hands the bestowal of the Kingdoms of this world, Edward III obtained the passsing of the Act of Provisors (1351), preventing the Pope appointing men to benefices during the lifetime of an incumbent, which was succeeded by the Acts of Praemunire of 1353 and 1392 aimed at withdrawal of the right of appeals from English Courts to that of Rome, and the final separation of the English Church from Papal jurisdiction in 1535.

A second cause was the revival of learning fostered by the teaching of the Friars, whose teaching of the principles of Roman Law, Natural Science, Medicine and Botany at Oxford, gave birth to the writings of the cynical William Langland, the courtly laughter-loving Geoffrey Chaucer, the moral Gower, the satirical Walter Mapes and, not the least, the philosophical Wycliffe who abjured the early teaching of philosophy to translate the Vulgate and organise his band of poor preachers.

In this book I have endeavoured to follow the history of the English Church from the Introduction of Christianity into the Island to the death of Wycliffe and, as I have no claim to bringing forward any original matter, but rather of treating the subject as a chronicle, I would acknowledge my indebtedness to the following Authors:

Lord Bryce: *The Holy Roman Empire.*

Dr. Burnett: *The History of the Reformation.*

Rev. Dr. Percy Dearmer: *Everyman's History of the Prayer Book.*

Rev. A. C. Law: *Illustrated Notes on Church History.*

John Stow: *Annals* and *Survey of London.*

Thomas Wright: *Vision and Creed of Piers Plowman.*

And I would above all express my thanks to the Rev. Herbert Browne (Rector of St. Lawrence, Newlands) for the encouragement he gave me to persevere in the production of the book.

WILLIAM HOWARD-FLANDERS

Latchingdon, Essex.

CONTENTS

PART ONE

CHAPTER ONE

CHAPTER TWO

CONTENTS

CHAPTER THREE

CHAPTER FOUR

CHAPTER FIVE

CHAPTER SIX

PART TWO

CHAPTER SEVEN

CHAPTER EIGHT

CHAPTER NINE

CHAPTER TEN

CHAPTER ELEVEN

PART ONE

INTRODUCTION

It is impossible to give any authentic account of the
Conversion of Britain. Some state that when Caradoc
(Caractacus) returned from Rome with his father, Cym-
beline, and his sister Morwena (Morgan la Feé), Pudens
and Claudia, he was accompanied by St. Paul (Pwl of the
Britons) who consulted Aaron (St. Eurien) as to the best
way of converting the inhabitants; others attribute it to
St. Joseph of Arimathea who, being banished from
Jerusalem after the Crucifixion, took ship with St. Philip,
Lazarus and Martha, at Marseilles, and landed on the
coast of South England, with him bringing two cruets
containing the Water and the Blood that flowed from the
Wounds of Christ and the blood-stained cloth (Sanguis
regalis) in a crystal vessel, afterwards known as the Holy
Grail, round which so many legends have been woven.
The petty king, Aviragus (who appears in some monkish
legends to have been confused with Arthur) gave these
pilgrims a piece of land in the Isle of Avalon, where
they dwelt in rough huts of wattle and built a chapel in
which they worshipped according to a primitive rite. This
may have been of oriental origin as the British Church
certainly worshipped in a manner different from that
introduced by St. Augustine.

he Diocletian persecution of the Claudian Nero was
moderated in Britain owing to the moderation of Constantine Chlorus who a local tradition says married

Helena, daughter of "Old King" Coel who ruled over the east of Britain; but, during this time, St. Alban was slain for having given shelter to, and exchanged clothes with, St. Amphibalus—a priest—at the place that still bears his name.

The British Church increased and was represented in the early Councils—Eborius of York, Restitutus of London, Adelphius of Civitas Coloniae (perhaps of Caerleon or Romsey), the priest Sacerdos and the deacon Arminius, being present at that of Arles (314). These prelates are said to have archbishops ruling over twenty-eight suffragans; at any rate, we have here evidence of the three orders. It was also represented at those of Nicæa (325), and Sardica (347) where they subscribed the Creed of St. Athanasius; but, at Rimini they were entrapped into admitting the teaching of Arius which was looked upon as unintentional as St. Hilary of Poitiers (356) said that, in spite of their wearing a crescent shaped tonsure, keeping Easter at a different date and practising only one immersion at baptism, they were free from any detestable heresy. St. Athanasius told Jovian (363) that they were loyal to the Catholic Faith; St. Jerome said that they worshipped the same Christ and observed the same rules of Faith as did other nations and St. Chrysostom declared that they discussed the Scripture in many tongues but with one spirit.

In the beginning of the fifth century, the Romans abandoned Britain, which was ravaged by the wild tribes of the North Sea and the Baltic.

Britain did not escape the stigma of heresy, and one Morgan (Pelagius or Water-borne) preached his doctrine concerning "Original Sin" to combat which the Council sitting at Troyes sent SS. Lupus and Germain to the Council of St. Albans.

The Picts and Scots broke over the Wall of Hadrian and ravaged Britain as far as Chester, where the Britons were advised by St. Germain to divide themselves into small bands and, hiding among the bushes near Flint, to utter simultaneous cries of "Hallelujah"! This frightened the enemy, who thought they were in greater strength than they really were.

When St. Germain returned to Gaul, he took with him many sons of the nobility, including Ninian—who went to Ireland, where he offended the King of Leitrim by preaching against the local industry—piracy—and, returning, built a church at "Whithern," known as the "White House"—Candida Casa.

St. Kentigern, who had already founded a monastery at St. Asaph (Llanwyg), built the Cathedral at Bangor (in the Gwynedd); Dubritius did the same at Llandaff (in the Morganwg), while St. David (a prince of the ruling house of the Brythons) preached to the Goidels of South Wales and moved his See from Caerleon to Menevia (Tyddewi now St. David's) in the Deheubarth.

During this period there is a break in historical facts in which the Chroniclers fitted into it the legend of King Arthur as the great Christian opponent to the heathen Saxon and Danes. He appears to have been a petty chieftain, and is known by the Briton as "Amberdan" (or Conqueror) and not as "Gwadeis" (or prince) and is described by Nennius as "dux bellorum". It is said that, while resting at Glastonbury, he had a vision directing him to worship in a little chapel known as the "Beckary", or "Hibernia", from having among its treasures the wallet, chaplet, bell and weaving stool of St. Bridget. Sir Gawain persuaded him to send his Chamberlain, who stole a silver candlestick, and was so severely wounded that he died on reaching the duke who, obeying the injunction, found the chapel guarded by four swords wielded by invisible hands. An aged priest, attended by the Virgin Mother (who acted as Acolyte), celebrated Mass and after offering the Holy Child,

B

he restored Him unhurt to His Mother, and received the silver Cross that he displayed as his ensign in his battles with the heathen.

The Saxons finding England richer than their own lands, settled in this country, founding the Kingdoms of Northumbria, East Anglia, Essex, Kent, Sussex and Mercia.

As a rule they avoided the walled cities, which they regarded as having been built by "negromancy" preferring to live in the open country, where they existed by means of the "Sortes Gothicœ"—that is living at free quarters and exacting two thirds of the produce of the land—and, while the Francs and Norsemen adopted the Romano Gallic language and customs, retained their own laws, language and religion, driving many of the British Christians to the mountains of the North and West, the forests of the Midlands and the Fens of the East. This was a matter of great importance as a broad land of heathenism separated them from their fellow Christians in France and Spain who remained in close communion with Rome.

CHAPTER ONE

THE MEDIAEVAL CHURCH

Jewish Observance—Services—Various Rulers—Ecclesiæ—Obedience to Rome—Celibacy—Holy Orders—Bishops—Universal Bishops—Episcopal Grades—Diocesan and Suffragan Bishops—Bishops in partibus —English Sees—Kent—Durham—Dorchester—Cornwall—Mercia— Lichfield—Coventry—Gloucester—Sodor and Man—Priests—Chauntry Priests—William Tyndale—Monastic Orders—Impropriated Parishes —Peculiars—Privileges of Clergy—Penance—Pilgrimages—Pardoners Sanctuaries—Cathedral Establishments—Collegiate Churches.

In order to make the change through which the Church passed, we will devote a few pages to the Rituals and Personnel of the Early Church.

The Christians naturally looked round them for some existing organisations whereon to model their form of worship, and found them in the Jewish observances and the existing Ecclesiæ.

In the first place, we find that Daniel is mentioned as praying with his face towards Jerusalem twice a day and both John and Peter went at the ninth hour to pray in the Temple. After the day of Pentecost, the members of the infant church were in the habit of meeting together on the eve of the Sabbath and prepared themselves for the celebration of the First day. This vigil was often long and wearisome, as we find that Eutychus was overwhelmed with fatigue and fell out of the window (Acts xx. 9). Later on, this service was divided into two parts—Evensong at dusk —Mattins at cockcrow—Lauds at Sunrise. Primes were followed at nine o'clock by Tierce at noon, Sext at three and Nones at six o'clock (often combined and celebrated as the Little Hours), while the day's Service ended with the Compline.

" And daily sacrifice be offered there
And Tierce and Nones and Mattins
Shall have each hallowed lay
And Angelus and Compline shall sweetly close each
  holy day."
                    —*Ecclesiologus*.—DR. MASON NEALE.

Later additions were the Little Hours of Our Lady, the Seven Penitential Psalms (VI, XXXIII, XXXVIII, LI, CII, CXXX and CXLIII) and the Rosary.

The various Churches had their own Liturgy of which the most important were:

I. An early Roman Ritual, probably founded on a lost Greek Rite;

II. The Syriac Rite of St. James;

III. The Egyptian Rite of SS. Mark, Basil, Gregory and Cyril;

IV. The Persian or Nestorian Rite, which gave rise to that of St. Thomas in India;

V. The Byzantine Rite of St. Chrysostom, Basil and Gregory Dialogos, being akin to the Greek Rite of Petrograd, in use among the Greek speaking inhabitants of the Western shore of the Adriatic (Magna Grecia) and is considered to be an Eastern Rite in a Western setting;

VI. The Gallican Rite (Spanish or Ephesian) attributed to St. John, who is said to have compiled it for the Ephesian Church whence it was introduced into Gaul by Irenaeus (Bishop of Lyon in the Second Century) who had been a disciple of Polycarp, who learned Christianity from the lips of St. John. It soon spread over Gaul to Italy (where it was suppressed by Charlemagne in favour of the Modern Roman Rite), Britain and Ireland.

VII. The Mozarabic Rite, either introduced by some Gothic Christians from Constantinople into Spain or a variation of the Gallican Rite which it so closely resembled that, when Charles the Bald wished to know more about the latter, he invited priests from Spain to rehearse its ritual. In the sixteenth century it was printed by order of Cardinal Zimines, who endowed a College of Priests at Toledo to perpetuate its existence.

VIII. The Ambrosian Rite is an adaption of Petrine —Hispano—Gallican Rite or an independent collation by St. Barnabas, and was preserved from extinction by the action of the patriotic clergy in the time of Charlemagne. It is now used by about a million Ambrosian Catholics in the north of Italy and was till lately used in the Ticine.

IX. The Modern Roman Rite has in most cases supplanted the others and gave rise to the Uses of Bangor, Hereford and Sarum. Collated with the Greek Ritual, it was used by the English Reformers in compiling the Book of Common Prayer.

The difference between these last two is unapparent to the ordinary hearer, and the writer was astonished when asked by a servant in Milan where she could find a Roman Catholic Church as she could only find those in which the Ambrosian Rite was used.

The early Christians sought to find some means of forming a religious fellowship and adopted that of Greek "ecclesiæ" or colleges founded for various purposes from those of worshipping some particular god, social intercourse, burial in some hallowed spot, insurance against fire or shipwreck, the return of certain political candidates, piratical expeditions or, even, the corruption of juries to obtain the discharge of felons, thus resembling in many ways benefit societies and clubs of modern days. Admission to these involved being elected, paying certain fees and giving a reception banquet. The chief officer was known as the Episcopus and, as the process of centralisation went on, one of these was chosen as the Archiepiscopus of the district.

Having described the growth of the Ritual and the formation of the Churches, we will go on to the personnel of the Early Church.

Looking towards Rome, we find that the keystone of the Church is obedience:

"Rome had spoken, it is useless to discuss it."

Another fundamental principle is celibacy of the clergy. This state of life was almost unknown in the Roman world, and till it was introduced into the West, when Alexander brought the eastern asceticism from Persia and thus laid the foundation of the Essenian doctrines that prevailed in Palestine at the period of the coming of St. John the Baptist.

Paul enjoined that bishops should be husbands of one wife and Calistus II (219–223) admitted married men to the priesthood and the episcopate; while the Apostolic Constitutions and Canons of the fourth century allowed married ecclesiastics to retain their wives but not to marry a second time. It was in the time of Siricius (305) that celibacy became compulsory even to the extent of priests renouncing their marriage vows, and Gregory VII insisted upon it, as we read:

"The holy Satan who made the wives
Of bishops lead such shameful lives."
            —*Golden Legend.*—LONGFELLOW.

But this was not always the case, and we read in "La Grande Italienne" (the Countess Matilda) written by René, that bishoprics in Lombardy were given as marriage portions ; and the bishopric of Coire was filled by hereditary right among the descendants of the Victorides. In 925, at Augsburg, it was decreed that the wives of priests were merely slaves. In Saxon England St. Dunstan was very severe towards married priests, and Lanfranc enforced celibacy upon the urban clergy. Gascoyne remarks that the bishop of St. David's lost over four hundred marks a year by refusing to grant licenses for the clergy to marry, and Canon Jessop, in his charming descriptions of English rural life, gives many instances of married priests and the fortunes of their wives. At the Councils of Constance and Bâle (1415 and 1439) attempts were made to legalise such marriages; but even the anti-Roman Elizabeth refused to acknowledge the rank of bishops' wives. Ferdinand, with the sovereigns of France, Poland and Bavaria, pleaded in vain for their recognition; but the Council of Trent refused to acknowledge the right of marriage. The question was raised by Joseph of Austria in 1782; and, in the dark days of the French Revolution, when the government not only allowed such marriages but looked upon unmarried priests as non-patriotic, but few ventured to disobey the Church.

In England we are accustomed to look upon holy Orders as being three in number; bishops, priests and deacons; but, in the Roman Church there are seven—bishops, priests, deacons, subdeacons, readers, exorcists and door-keepers.

The highest rank in the Ecclesiastical hierarchy is that of bishop whose functions are those of ordaining deacons and priests, consecrating churches, confirming candidates for Church Membership and generally supervising the discipline of the clergy in their dioceses. In the Roman Church the Pope is the chief authority, being the "Pontifex Maximus", the representative of the Chief of the College of "Pontifices" who supervised public worship from the earliest days of Rome. Julius Cæsar annexed this office to that of Emperor, and the two dignities were united till the latter was abandoned by Gratian. He is frequently spoken of as Servus Servorum Ecclesiæ Christi, Patriarch of Rome and of the West, Primate of Italy and Head of the Universal Church.

Originally all bishops were equal, but the First Council of Nicæa gave weight to the opinion of those of Rome, Alexandria, Constantinople and Jerusalem; the Second Council decreed that all questions would be settled by the bishop of the diocese and the African prelates declared that there was no right of appeal to Rome; but the Third and Fourth Councils gave precedence to those of Rome and Constantinople as being representatives of the two seats of the Empire.

Cyprian and the early bishops addressed him as "fellow bishop", "colleague" and "friend"; and so far from allowing to any prelate the title of Universal bishop, when Mauritus granted that title to the Eastern Patriarch which was opposed by Gregory I (500) as being a sign of "Luciferian pride", declaring any one accepting it to be "anti-Christ"; but, Boniface II (530) accepted it at the hands of Justinian and the eighth of that name (1294) claimed to have the bestowal of the Universal Kingdom and Universal jurisdiction in all matters—Spiritual and Temporal.

In the Roman Church there are several grades in the Episcopal ranks—Patriarchs, Primates, Archbishops, Diocesan Bishops and Bishops in Partibus Infidelium. In England we have only Primates and Archbishops, Diocesan, Suffragan and Co-adjutor Bishops. The first two are the Chief Ecclesiastical Authorities in either province with seats of power at Canterbury and York. The function of the Diocesan Bishops are to ordain priests and deacons, license lay readers, confirm candidates for Church Membership and consecrate churches. They are assisted by archdeacons, many of whom are consecrated as suffragans.

In the Middle Ages there were many bishops in Partibus Infidelium, most of whom had been driven from their dioceses by the Turks; and, later, the title was given to those bishops in those countries in which the Roman hierarchy was declared to be illegal, as in England, till the repeal of the Ecclesiastical Tithes Act in 1871. Thus we read in the lines of Piers Plowman:

" And prelates that he maketh
That bear bishops' names
Of Bethelehem and Babiloign
That huppe aboute in Engelonde
To halwe[1] mennes auteres
And amonge curatours
And confessen ayen the lawe."
—*Vision.*—10696–10703.

Under the Roman Empire, the boundaries of the See were coterminous with those of the provinces, and this was followed to a large extent by the Anglo-Saxon episcopate.

Kent was divided into two Sees, those of Canterbury and Rochester: the latter representing the obscure Kingdom of West Kent. The See of London included the City, Essex, Middlesex and Hertfordshire.

In 1541, Westminster was separated from it, but only had one bishop (Thirlby) who surrendered it on accepting that of Norwich. In 1865, Essex was included in that of Rochester, and in 1875 in that of St. Albans, while

[1] Hellow.

the See of Chelmsford was erected in 1908, having at the time of writing 600 parishes; 700 clergy, and over a million of lay inhabitants.

In 684, Egfrith granted land in Durham to St. Cuthbert of Lindisfarne, and in 875, when the See of Lichfield was removed to Chester-le-Street, Guthrum the Dane endowed the church at Durham with lands lying between the Tees, the Tyne and Watling Street. When the Danes pushed on to Chester (995) the monks removed the body of St. Cuthbert to the college of Durham, of which Edmond was the first bishop. Another bishop—Walcher—purchased the earldom of Durham and Carlief (1068) and built the Benedictine monastery; another, Pudsey, obtained the earldom of Sedburgh, which had hitherto formed a distinct jurisdiction (1155); and, till 1831, the Bishop of Durham was a lay peer as well as a prelate, and as such could sit in Court when there was a question of life and death. In 1295 the bishops were in possession of the rights of regalia over Norhamshire, Bedlingtonshire, Hexhamshire, Islandshire, Carlisle (till 1541), Crayle and part of Teviotdale as Earls Palatine. In the reign of Edward VI, the Duke of Northumberland (Dudley) obtained the deprivation of Tonstall in hopes of founding a vast principality in the north. The privileges of the county palatine were curtailed in 1596, abolished in 1648, restored in 1660, and annexed to the Crown in 1836.

Dorchester was an extensive See at one time, extending from the Wash to the Thames and as far as the confines of Devonshire. During the lifetime of Agilbert (636) Winchester was given to Wini and (678) Eadhus moved the episcopal See to Lindissa and Ethelwine to Sidnacester. In 1072, Regimus the Bishop (formerly almoner of Fêcamp) removed it to Lincoln where it has since remained. It lost Ely in 1004 and Medehampstead (Peterborough) and Bedford in 1541.

In the time of Solomon, king of Cornwall, that county was evangelised by Corantinus whose work was continued by St. Paran—(commemorated by the ruined church of Perranzabuloe St. Perran in the sands) about 450. St. Petroe was bishop of Bodmin (about 800) and had thirteen successors, some of whom had their Sees at Germaines, which See was acquired by Lyvyngus of Crediton who thus became Bishop of Cornwall. In 1840, Leofric transferred the See to Exeter where Edward the Confessor sent monks from Westminster.

Mercia had several Sees—Lichfield, Coventry, Hereford, Worcester, Gloucester, and Leicester.

Lichfield (656, often joined to Coventry) was founded for Duma in 656 ; and Offa, being the most powerful king of the Heptarchy, jealous of the supremacy of Canterbury, obtained the pall for Bishop Higbert who was appointed by the Council of Chelsea (787) as arch-bishop over the five Sees of Mercia and the two in East Anglia—Dunwich and Elmham; but his successor—Adulph—was relieved of this charge. In 1075, Bishop Peter removed his See to Chester-le-Street (and before the Reformation we hear of the Bishop of "Chester") and afterwards to Coventry (1102) which church was subject to Lichfield whither Hugh de Novant returned in 1148. Although the See bore a double name it was but one, as the bishop was chosen alternately by the regulars of Lichfield and the seculars of Coventry.

Walter Froudester was made mitred Abbot of Gloucester which was separated from Worcester in 1841 and since then has frequently been held with that of Bristol.

The Bishop of Sodor and Man holds an anomalous position. He has never been recognised as a peer of Parliament, having been (till recently) appointed by the titular King of Man. Some say that the first Bishop of Man was Aumphibalus and others that the See was provided by St. Patrick who made Germain as the first bishop in 447. Sodor was made a bishopric in 1099 by Magnus of Norway who united it to that of Man. The bishops subsequently owed allegiance to the "Kings of Man"; the Earls of Salisbury (1343), were succeeded by those Earls of Northumberland and of Derby and the dukes of Atholl, from whom the regalian rights were purchased by the Crown in 1829.

By far the greater number of clerks in holy orders are the priests set aside by episcopal ordination to administer the Sacraments, conduct public worship and teach the people of their respective parishes; being distinguished from the deacons who have no authority to officiate at the Holy Communion or to give absolution.

In the Middle Ages the priests were all powerful in the State as well as in the Parish, as they were almost the only persons who could read or write. We shall have occasion to see how they served the King in matters of State; but now, we will examine the position of the priest—parochial or otherwise. One means of their gaining their great influence over the people was by settling disputes which might otherwise have come before the Court baron of the manor, or even before the King's Court—a practice keenly protested against by lawyers who accuse them of perverting the will of Justice and enriching themselves.

> " Wisdom and wit now
>   Is not worth a kers
>   And clotheres combe hem welle
>   Who so can contreve deceites
>   And ledeth forth a love day—
>   To lette with Truthe,
>   He that swiche[1] craftes can[2]
>   To counseil is cleped[3].
>
> —*Vision.*—5628–37.

[1] Such.   [2] Knows.   [3] Called.

The superior position in which the clergy were placed caused many to seek orders, and as there were more priests than parishes they were fain to hang about the various churches in hopes of being engaged to sing Masses at the tombs of the departed. It is not within our province to discuss the question of Masses for the Dead; we must therefore content ourselves with stating that these men were not always of the brightest examples of intellectual attainments or morality.

In 1363, the Commons complained that "Chapelleines sont devenues si chers" that they demanded and obtained ten or twelve marks (say £6 13s. 4d. or £8) "a grant grievances du peple" and Islip ordered that "no more should be given to priest for their yeerely stipend than three pounds six shillings and eightpence which caused many of them to steale."—ANNALES.

They appear to have been divided into two classes: "Chapelleines pariochiels" who might receive six marks (£4 2s. 0d.) and "Chapelleines chantanz annueles et a cure des almes nient entendenz," who might receive five marks (£3 18s. 8d.). Later (1414) the stipend of "Chapelleine Parochiel" was raised to eight marks (£5 6s. 8d.) and that of "annueller" to seven (£4 13s. 4d.).

These men often lodged at the house of a layman who may have helped them to eke out their pittance by employing them as clerks and stewards as we read in Chaucer:

"In London was a preest, an annullere,
　That therein dwelt hadde many a yere
　Which was so plesant, and so serviceable
　Unto the wif, thereas he was at table
　That she would suffre him nothing to pay
　For borde ne clothing, went he never so gay."
　　　　　　　—*Canterbury Tales.*—16479–16484.

There was in the sixteenth century a notable priest —William Tyndale—who, seeing there was "no room in

the palace of the Bishop of London or in all England"
to translate the Bible, obtained a post of chauntry priest
in the Church of St. Dunstan's in the West to pray for
the souls of the father and mother of Master Monmouth
and lived in the house of his patron, "passing his time
as a good priest should, studying his book, and eating of
his own free will nothing but sodden meat and poor
ale."

Towards the end of the second century, men and
women saw the necessity of leaving fashionable life—full
of luxury and vice—in order to work out their own
salvation by good works and meditation in the sandy
wastes of Egypt.

About the year A.D. 270 one of these, St. Anthony,
lived a solitary life in the Fayoum, gained such a reputation for holiness and wisdom that many of both sexes
appealed to him for guidance, and he divided them
into small communities of three or more. It is impossible
for us in the twentieth century to imagine through what
hardships they passed.

St. Benedict re-organised these Communities and taught
men and women of gentle birth to live the "outward life
of a beast and the inner life of an angel" by praying
and working, fasting and meditating, taking as recreation
manual labour for abbot and monk and serving men
alike. It was rarely that the brethren were in major
orders; but at the Council of Constantinople (445) we
read of many monks being in full orders. There was
continual strife between abbots and bishops and at the
Council of Arles (656) Faustus of Lerins claimed to be
independent of all control. To end this, Justinian ordered
that all abbots should be subject to the bishop of the
diocese. Although St. Bernard protested against them
exercising episcopal authority and wearing episcopal
insignia, Alexander II (1063) granted to the Abbot of
Canterbury the right to wear mitre, gloves, ring and

sandals and to carry a pastoral staff with the crook directed inwards to show that his jurisdiction was confined to his precincts.

From small beginnings the monasteries increased in numbers and in wealth, and in many cases, claiming exemption from regal and episcopal control, became a power in the land. The great increase in wealth made rivals of the parochial clergy, and as they received many churches through benefactions, the parishes were often badly served by ill-paid chaplains and vicars, a practice that accounts for the poverty of many English benefices.

About 1180, Robert Mantell founded a Praemonstratensian abbey at Beleigh to which he gave the two churches of All Saints and St. Peter (Maldon). According to custom the convent served these churches by means of a chaplain who was removable at pleasure and enjoyed none of the privileges of an incumbent. The Lateran Council of 1215 decreed that all impropriated parishes should be served by a vicar who should be allowed "an honourable and sufficient income" out of the church. In 1244, Fulke Basset, of London, united the two parishes on account of their "leanness and poverty," retaining All Saints as the mother church with the offerings of the two parishes, except the tythe of corn, the vicar paying to the abbey two and a half marks in silver (33s. 4d.) at Easter and Michaelmas, and all dues and customary payments (except the episcopal and archidiaconal procurations), in return for which, the abbey handed over to the vicarage the house in a good state of repair.

On the death of Ferroby, the convent acted as patrons till the Dissolution, since when it has passed through many hands till it was given to the bishop of the diocese. At the Reformation, the church of St. Peter fell into decay and was converted by Dr. Plume (Archdeacon of Rochester) into a library and school.

Close by are two parishes which suffered much at the Dissolution, Steeple, in the gift of Stansgate priory, passed into private hands, and all that remains of its benefactions are the small tythes amounting to something like £104 a year!

In the neighbouring parish of Mayland, the greater tythes, something like £411, were granted to St. Bartholomew's Hospital; the vicar received the smaller tythes (about £122 a year) and at Purleigh, the advowson was in the hands of the priory of Norton and passed into private hands till it was purchased to augment the Mastership of Oriel College. In 1881, the tythes were divided, one half going to the Master, and the other half to the Rector. All these benefices are in Essex.

The wealthy Benedictine House of St. Mary, at York, possessed many impropriated rectories which it administered by means of vicars. Among these is that of Kirkby Lonsdale, which at the Dissolution was valued at £1,300, of which £1,000 went to the Court of Augmentations and was given by Mary to Trinity College (Cambridge), and the £300 was left to the vicar.

Scattered over the county are many benefices in the gift of the Archbishop of Canterbury, and those of Essex were placed under the jurisdiction of the joint deans of Bocking, one of whom resides in that parish and the other at Hadleigh, in Suffolk.

The early Christians settled their disputes among themselves and, as the Church grew stronger, the clerics claimed exemption from the imperial courts. This tended to increase their numbers until it included not only bishops, priests and deacons, but readers, exorcists, door-keepers, students, pilgrims, palmers, summoners and pardoners to such an extent that Gibbon mentions six thousand "parabolani" and eleven thousand "copiatae" whose duties seem to have been to attend the sick and bury the dead in Constantinople.

In the Saxon time, the bishops were present in the County Courts till William I. gave them great power in those of the Church, and, as we shall see when treating of the times of Becket, they claimed exceptional privileges. Later they arrogated to themselves these privileges to all who could read or write or recite the "neck verse" which is variously given

> Dominus pars hereditatis
> meæ—*Psalm* lv. 1.
> Is a murie [1] verset.

> " It hath taken from Tybourne
> Twenty strong theeves;
> There lewed[2] theeves ben lolled up
> Lok how thei ben saved."
> —*Vision.*—7892–7896.

And again

"Have mercy upon us, God; according to Thy loving-kindness; according to the multitude of Thy mercies blot out our transgression."—*Psalm* li. 1.

After establishing his claim for the benefit of clergy by reading the required verse, the condemned person was branded on the hand, and, to this day the culprit is required to hold up his hand when pleading to show the Court that he has not been previously convicted. In 1487 this privilege was extended to all peers, whether they could read and write or not, and to women in 1622. The last time it was claimed was by the Duchess of Kingston, on her conviction for felony in 1776, and it was abolished in 1827.

In the days of the later Roman Empire the rigorous code of morality professed by the Christians grew lax, and voluntary confession gave place to an inquisitorial

---

[1] Merry.   [2] Common.

c

examination by the priest. In the time of Charlemagne, the clergy were in possession of a secret code of offences and their punishment. The more ordinary crimes of murder, rapine, perjury and theft were punishable by sentences of excommunication, involving exclusion from the Court and the battlefield for periods easily amounting to one hundred years and more, by which the King would lose the services of his vassal, perhaps in the times when they were most needed. This form of punishment was therefore commuted into a monetary payment of from three to twenty-six Solidi (9s.: £3 18s. 0d.), according to the magnitude of the offence and the position of the guilty one for each offence. As this might involve a debt of something like £13,000 and might involve the alienation of an estate to wipe out a penitential period of three hundred years, St. Dominic Loricatus devised a system by which the person of the condemned might suffer instead of his estate, and he became so skilful that he could inflict three hundred stripes in six days.

Another way of expiating sin was to go on a pilgrimage, and in the second century of our era the principal pilgrim resorts were places connected with the Life and Passion of Our Lord. Later, vast crowds went to visit the tombs of the Apostles and the Early Martyrs at Rome, the Holy House of Lorette, Assisi, Compostella, Montserrat, St. Denis, Cettin, Zell, Einsiedeln, Walsingham, Canterbury and many other places. Those who went to the Holy Land were given letters of introduction to the commanders of the Templars and Knights Hospitallers, and frequently performed their journey under severe conditions. In the "Vita Liudgari," we read how a fratricide travelled having round his loins a heavy chain which burst asunder when he knelt before the shrine of that saint.

Theoderet mentions the practice of leaving votive gifts, such as the models of hands, feet and ears in gold, silver or wax, by those who had benefited by such an act of devotion. On their return they frequently bore in their hats small leaden representations of the keys of Rome, the Vernicle, the Head of St. Thomas of Canterbury, the scallopshell of St. James, or small leaden vessels (ampullae) containing water from some holy spring.

Palmers differed from pilgrims as they were vowed to spend a certain time, during which they had to live on charity, in the Holy Land.

Like many travellers of the present day—

> " Pilgrims and Palmeres
> Plyghten[1] hem togidere
> For to seken saint Jame
> And seintes at Rome,
> That wenten forth in hire way
> With many wise tales
> And hadden leve to lyen
> Al hire lif after. "
>
> *—Vision.—*91–98.

> " His sele shold noght be sent
> To deceyve the people."
>
> *—Vision.—*130–160.

Later on, Chaucer also speaks of the "pardoner" who had with him a wallet containing among other sacred objects "alle hote from Rome " a "pilwe bere made from Our Lady's veil, " a "gobbet of the sail of St. Peter's boat when he was saved from shipwreck by Christ"; a cross of "laten ful of stones " and "pigges bones in a glas".

> " A poure parson dwelling up in lond,
> Upon a day he get more monie
> Than the persone gat in monthes twei."

[1] Pledge.

" He was in churche a noble ecclesiast,
  Wel coude he rede a lesson or a storie;
  And alderbeste he sang an offertorie
  For wel he wiste[1] that when that songe was songe
  He must preche and well affile his tonge,
  To winnen silver as he right wel coude
  Therfore he sang the merrier and loude."
                    —*Canterbury Tales.*—671.

Not only did the clergy enjoy exemption from the ordinary course of criminal law, but also claimed exemption from the execution of the King's writs in respect to the ecclesiastical buildings and even over Church lands. This was based upon the regulation in Leviticus IV, which gave an accused person the opportunity to escape from the vengeance of an infuriated mob and was copied by the Roman Church. Most of the monasteries, such as Westminster, St. Albans, Durham, Bury and the White- and Black- Friars, together with the precincts of the royal palaces, the Savoy, the Mints on Tower Hill and in Southwark, St. Martin's le Grand, St. Katherine, Fullwood's Rents, Baldwin's Gardens and Salisbury and Mitre Courts enjoyed this privilege. With the exception of White Friars (where the ordinary writs, unless signed by the Lord Chief Justice, had no effect till 1697), these rights were swept away at the Dissolution and seven other places were substituted—Wells, Westminster, Northampton, Manchester (replaced by Chester), Derby and Launceston. The grants of sanctuary usually followed something after this wording "that any fugitive from justice of whatsoever condition, suspected of any crime whatsoever and coming from any place whatsoever, should be received, and any one who should attempt to interfere with his liberty should lose his name, worship,

[1] Knew.

power and dignity and with the traitor Judas, the betrayer of Our Lord, be cast into the everlasting fires of Hell ".

In order to avail himself of safety, the fugitive had to present himself at an early hour before the King's coroner who would direct him to abjure the realm and leave it by the shortest route to the nearest seaport, unless ordered to do otherwise. In case of disobedience, he was liable to arrest and trial in the ordinary course.

Boniface VIII (1487) expressly forbade this benefit to any one who had escaped from custody or had committed a fresh offence since seeking sanctuary.

Having thus far treated of the personnel of the Church, we will look at the buildings used for its services. They may be described as Cathedrals, Collegiate Churches and Parish Churches. The collegiate church of Westminster is frequently styled cathedral, perhaps, because there was one bishop of that short-lived diocese, and at Bath and Wells and at Ipswich and Bury there are cathedrals; in mediaeval times, the large churches employed a great number of hands. The bishop had but little to do with his cathedral (having on his consecration to knock for admittance) besides occupying the throne and sometimes acting as visitor, the charge of the building being vested in the dean, who is the head of the Chapter. Previous to the Reformation the prior acted as dean in the monastic Cathedrals and was assisted by the precentor who has the custody of the church and arranges the musical services with the aid of the succentor. The chancellor is secretary of the Chapter, presides over the Church courts and superintends the library and schools. The canons take part in the service and are residentiary or non-residentiary; in the latter case, they are represented by their vicars choral who sit in the stalls immediately under their principals. In St. Paul's there are besides the thirty canons, twelve minor canons who form a distinct college under the senior cardinal; fifty chauntry priests;

thirty Vicars and many minor officials such as the Sacristan with his three vergers, the masters of singing and grammar schools; the almoner and his four vergers; servitors; surveyors; scribes; book-binders; chamberlain; rent-collectors; brewers (in 1287 no less than 67,814 gallons of beer were brewed); sextons; gravediggers; gardeners; bakers (who baked as many as 11,000 loaves in one year); bell ringers; maker and menders of robes; cleaners; sweepers; carpenters; masons; carvers; and gilders; in all some hundreds of persons were employed in carrying on public worship in the great cathedral in London. And the same in the other cathedrals.

A second class of churches are those known as "collegiate", being served by a number of priests under the supervision of a dean or master. Of these we will take a list from *Crockford*:

Brecon: with seven prebends—all vacant;

St. Endillion: a rectory and seven prebends;

Eton: a provostry and ten fellowships, the holders of which are not necessarily in holy orders, but act as governors of the school;

Heytesbury: a rectory and three prebends—all vacant;

St. Katherine's (now in Regent's Park): with a master, five members of the chapter, sisters and two chaplains.

Wimbourne (formerly a chapel royal): a deanery and four canons and a vicar of peculiars abolished in 1843;

Windsor: a deanery and four canonries and a college of poor knights;

Wolverhampton: a rectory. Formerly there was a deanery frequently held with that of Windsor till, on the death of Dean Hobart (1846), it was abolished, together with the prebends;

Westminster: a deanery, four canonries, five minor canonries and forty king's scholars.

CHAPTER TWO

THE ANGLO-SAXON CHURCH

Anglo Saxon Churches—St. Augustine—Celtic and Gallican Churches—
Sees of London—Northumbria—East Anglia—Lindisfarne—Council
of Whitby—Succession to York—Aglbert and Wini—Cedd—Wilfrid
—Theodore at Canterbury—Tythes—Learned Prelates—King Alfred
—Odo of Canterbury—Dunstan—St. Alphage and the Sack at Canterbury—Edward the Confessor—Foreign Bishops—Harold—Conquest
of England.

ENGLAND might have remained in a state of heathen
darkness had not Ethelbert of Kent married Bertha—
the daughter of Charibert (King of Paris), who stipulated
that she should be allowed freedom of worship under the
direction of Bishop Luidhard.

The popes had had their eyes upon England and
Gregory I, thinking of reviving the hierarchy with metro-
politans at London and York, sent St. Augustine and
forty companions to accomplish the task. When these
men heard of the cruelties of the Saxon kings at the
monastery at Lerins several of them refused to go on, but
Augustine continued his journey and landed at Ebbesfleet,
in the Isle of Thanet. Ethelbert, who was doubtless
aware of the miracles wrought by Christ, which he put
down in his ignorance, to witchcraft, refusing to meet
Augustine under a roof, selecting the shade of an oak
tree as the scene of a conference. The result was that he
gave to the missionary the ruined churches of St. Martin,
St. Mary in the Castle, St. Pancras and the church in the
Palace, which was re-dedicated to "Our Holy Saviour and

God, our Lord Jesus Christ" and was baptised with his court on the following Whit-Sunday (597).

Augustine knew of the British Church and invited the monks of Bangor and Caerleon on Usk to meet him under an oak at Aust. Taking care to be seated when they arrived, his omission to rise to greet them caused them to say he was not "meek and lowly of heart, but stern and proud and not of God". They were willing to agree with him upon many points, but differed upon those of the triple immersion at baptism and the date of the observance of Easter, which was caused rather by the disorder that had crept into their calendar from a question of doctrine, and declared that while they were willing to owe fraternal love to all the Church of God and all Christians, they could not acknowledge the authority of him whom Augustine called the Pope of Rome, as they were already bound in canonical obedience to the Archbishop of Caerleon.

Some blame Augustine for not translating the Liturgy into the vernacular Saxon, but he did wisely in continuing the services in Latin as the Saxon dialects varied considerably from each other; but, had he done so, he would have created a merely local Saxon Church and have cut off England from the rest of Europe.

Being only a Benedictine abbot, he was unable to perform any episcopal duties, and went to Gaul where he was consecrated as Bishop of the Angles (and not of England, which gave him no authority over the scattered British Christians) by Æthurius of Lyons and Virgilius of Arles (602), and did not receive the pall till it was sent by Gregory at the hands of Justin, Mellitus and Paulinus with the necessary sacred vessels.

The first was consecrated to Rochester and the second to London, receiving from Ethelred the manor of Tillingham.

Knowing that his end was fast approaching, Augustine consecrated his friend Laurentius as his successor, which was a distinctly uncanonial act as the Council of Antioch (364) forbade any bishop consecrating his successor, and that of Nicæa decreed that no bishop should hold more than one See at the same time; but the dying man, anxious that the infant English Church should suffer no drawback, risked the danger of doing so lest a moment's interregnum should bring it to harm.

Laurentius invited the British bishops, whom he addressed as "most dear lords and brethren", to a conference; but this, too, proved a failure, as the Benedictine monks laughed and jeered at their quaint habits, their Celtic tonsures and their long beards.

Sebert of the East Saxons willingly received Mellitus, and gave him land upon which was afterwards erected St. Paul's and St. Peter's (Westminster) in 604, on the Island of Thorney and the manor of Tillingham. He removed the heathen symbols from the Saxon temples. On his death, his sons refused to be baptised and drove out the Bishop as he would not allow them to partake of the "white bread", that is the Sacrament (616). Redwald of East Anglia merely tolerated Christianity.

Ethelbert was succeeded by his son, Eadbald, who remained a pagan and persecuted Justin of Rochester (translated to Canterbury in 624), to such an extent that he would have fled had he not dreamed that St. Peter threatened him with a sound flogging if he showed such cowardice.

The evangelisation of Kent was followed by that of the other extreme of England—Northumbria—as Eadbald would only allow Edwin to marry his sister Ethelburga on his agreeing to allow her the same privileges as her mother had enjoyed, and she was accompanied to the north by Paulinus, to whom Edwin gave a piece of ground upon which a church (afterwards York Minster) was erected. Then at the meeting of the Northumbrian Witan, the high priest declared that the worship of the

White Christ could not be less profitable to the kingdom than that of Wodin had been, and many nobles welcomed the Teaching of Paulinus as to the future existence. The heathen temples were destroyed and on Easter Eve (627) Edwin and a thousand of his nobles were baptised; but before Paulinus could receive the pall the King was slain by the heathen Penda of Mercia, and Ethelburga (accompanied by her son Oswine and Paulinus, who took with him the sacred vessels) had to flee to Kent.

Siegeric of East Anglia and his brother, Eorpwald, had to flee to Gaul, where the former was baptised and, returning, obtained the help of the Burgundian, Felix, to preach to the people.

This Apostle of East Anglia took up his residence at Dunwich, of which "honest" John Stow speaks of having "two hundred and fifty divine houses and parish churches or hospitals and chapels and as manie windmills and as manie toppe shippes . . . even of late times there were within the sayde toune six parish churches, two houses of Friars, an house which had been of Templars, two hospitals and three chapelles, foure of these parish churches are now of late swallowed up by the sea, and two of them remaining on the land, to wit, Saint Peter's and All Saints. The men of Dunwich desiring succour for their toune against the rage of the seas, affirm that a great piece of the Forest, sometime thereby is devoured and turned to the use of the sea. Felix their first bishop sate 18 yeeres and ended his life there in anno 649 and was buried at Soham, a place where sometimes a great famous monasterie stoode replenished with religious persons, under their Abbot Warfred, which house was founded by a nobleman named Lutinges, and wholly subverted by the Danes; and the body of Felix was removed to Romsey, where Felix founded a church at Radham which was also destroyed by the Danes. Felix also founded schools—at Felixtow, now called Filchstow.

After Felix succeeded Thomas, a deacon borne in Essex, he sate five yeeres. After him Brigildis surnamed Boniface, a Kentish man borne who sate seventeen yeeres. After him succeeded Bisi who divided it into two Byshoryke, to wit, Dunwich and Elmham. Thus much for Dunwich."—ANNALES.

The monks of Canterbury were much disturbed by Felix being helped by a Scots monk named Fursey, who followed the Celtic rite, but they could do nothing, as their jurisdiction did not extend beyond Kent.

Edwin's predecessor, Ethelfrith, left three sons (Oswold, Oswine and Oswy) who fled to Iona, where the first thought more of regaining his father's kingdom than of following the teaching of the monks and, defeating the Welsh, became King of Northumbria, but was slain by Penda, and Oswine obtained Beira and Oswy Bernicia.

During the Civil war that ensued, Oswine was slain, and Oswy became King of United Northumbria. Knowing that the recall of Paulinus would mean the return of Ethelburga and her son, Oswine, he applied to the monks of Iona who sent St. Aidan, who (as Paulinus was still bishop of York) fixed his See at Lindisfarne, where he quickly gathered round him the sons of the chief men of the north, whom he employed in translating and illuminating the Vulgate and other Church books.

Aidan was succeeded by Finan (651) and Colman (662) and, as Oswy had married Eanfleda (daughter of Edwin and Ethelburga) who had her children baptised by her Chaplain, Wilfrid, trouble broke out in the Church, especially concerning the date of Easter, to solve which the King summoned the Council known as that of Whitby-Streanaeshalc, at which were present himself, Colman, Cedd (Bishop of London) and Hilda, the Abbess, represented the Celtic School, and the Queen and her son

Alfric, Agilbert of Dorchester, the priest, Agathus, and Romanus, the deacon, the Gallicans.

When Colman defended the observance of Easter on the fourteenth day of the Paschal moon, Wilfrid said that was a local concession made by St. John for the Church of Ephesus, and that the obscure Britons and Picts could not maintain their local traditions when opposed to the teaching of Rome; and Oswy decided against him when he could not maintain that the gift of the "keys" had been made to St. Columba as he feared to offend St. Peter lest he should be refused admission to Paradise. Seeing all was lost, the Celtic Bishop resigned his See and took the body of St. Cuthbert to Chester-le-Street. When the Danes plundered that town in 995, the monks removed the body to Durham, where Egfrid had granted land to St. Cuthbert.

Wilfrid refused to take Lindisfarne as the seat of his authority (which he considered to be at York) and went to Compeigne, where he was consecrated by twelve bishops, who rejoiced at the victory of Whitby.

Pope Honorius (626) had granted to the Burgundian, Birinius, leave to preach Christianity in those parts of England untouched by the mission of St. Augustine. Having been consecrated by Listerius of Genoa, he arrived in England in 635 and gaining the favour of Cynegeles of Wessex, baptised him (Oswald of Northumbria being one of his sponsors), and received a piece of ground upon which he built the Abbey Church of Dorchester, the seat of the largest See in the country, as it extended from the Wash to the Thames and the confines of Devonshire. His son—Cenwalch—was adverse to Christianity; and after having driven its supporter across the Parret, had to seek safety with Anna of East Anglia, where he was converted.

Returning, he found that Birinius had been succeeded by Agilbert, who was ignorant of the Wessex dialect, and built another church at Winchester, where he placed the Bishop, Wini, who went abroad for consecration. Agilbert was displeased at this decision, and again went abroad, and died Bishop of Paris. Eadus (678) removed the See of Dorchester to Lindissa, and, two years later, Ethelwine became Bishop of Sidnaceaster.

Death was busy with the episcopal bench. Deusdedit of Canterbury, Cedd of London, Damian of Rochester, and Tuda of Lindisfarne all died between 655 and 668.

Of Cedd we will borrow a few lines from Stowe, who thus describes him—"an holie man—who did mightily beate downe errours and wanne many by preaching the christian religion in his dominions. Thereupon Cedd was by Finan consecrated Bishoppe of the East Saxons, and then proceeded with more authoritie in his function, ordering priests and deacons in all places of Essex, but especially in Ithancester and Tilburie. The citie of Ithancester, stoode on the banke of the riuer Pante that runneth by Maldune in the Hundred of Danseye, but now that Citie is drowned in Pante, so that nothing remaineth but the ruines of the citie in the said riuer".—ANNALES.

As Wilfrid still remained abroad without making any provision for the management of his See, Chadd of Lastingham (brother to Cedd) was appointed to take his his position. Going to Canterbury to seek consecration at the hands of Deusdedit, he found that he had died, and then went on to Winchester where, as the Council of Nicæa ordained that three bishops should assist at such a ceremony, Wini obtained the help of Celtic prelates.

Egbert of Kent and Oswy of Northumbria wished to have an Englishman as primate and sent Vighard to Rome for consecration, but as he died before he could receive the pall, Vitalian selected a monk of Tarsus—Theodore—as his successor. He found that there were but few prelates in England, including Chadd, whom he liked and Wilfrid whom he disliked, and, in spite of his

spirit of toleration, removed the first from York on account
of the irregularity of his consecration, although he afterwards made him bishop of Lichfield. His impartiality
was shown by the appointment of the Gallicans Putta,
Acci and Heddi to Rochester, Norfolk and Wessex and
the Celtic Eata, Trumbert, Bosa, Saxwulph and Cuthbert
to Hexham, Lichfield and Lindisfarne.

He reformed the episcopate by dividing East Anglia
into Elmham and Dunwich; Wessex into Winchester and
Sherborne and Mercia into Lichfield, Hereford, Leicester
and Lindsey.

Wilfrid allowed Bosa to exercise episcopal functions
in York, and travelled about England forming churches
(among which were those of Hexham and Ripon), restored
discipline in the monasteries and reformed Church music.
He went as far south as Sussex, where he taught the
inhabitants of the coast to mitigate a famine by adding
sea-fishing to their occupations. Receiving land from
Eadwald, he built a monastery at Selsey, which was
removed to Chichester.

Being reinstated in York, he regained his influence, till
he was banished for advising the Queen to retire into a
nunnery.

Theodore then divided York into the Sees of Lindisfarne, Hexham and Whithorne, against which Wilfrid
appealed to Pope Agathus (679) who, only too pleased
to be able to interfere in English church matters, summoned a Council of Bishops who absolved him on all
counts, and invited him to be present at another, in
which he styled himself as "Wilfrid, Bishop of the City
of York", who having appealed to the Apostolic See and
having been absolved from all blame and charges,
definite and indefinite, was placed on the judgment seat
with one hundred and twenty-five other bishops and
confessed the "True and Catholic Faith for all the Northern
Regions, that is the lands of Britain and Ireland besides

that of the Picts and Scots". Thus, he asserted a harmony between the Celtic and Gallic schools that did not exist. Bosa was elected to supersede him (678) and remained at York for eight years.

As Theodore travelled about the country with his friend, the Abbot Hadrian, he persuaded many of the landowners to build churches in their manors and endow them with funds (tythes) and lands (glebes) for the support of the maintenance of the bishop, priest, fabric and poor; but in England they do not appear (according to Lord Selborne) to have been used for the maintenance of the building, which is in the care of the church-wardens (and now of the Church council) or for the relief of the poor. They were ordered to be paid by the Synod and treaty of Wedmore (786-798) and by the laws of Athelstane, Edgar and Alfred (910–1033).

Tythes are "predial" (arising from arable, pasture and woodland); "mixed" (from cattle, swine, eggs, etc.); "personal" (from mills and places of industry) and "little" from house rents (as at Winchelsea and in the deanery of Battle). In many London parishes there is a tythe rate in lieu of tythes. Except by custom there is no tythe on barren land, minerals, wild and tame animals (except cattle) or from glebe lands in the hands of the incumbent.

After Rosa had ruled York for eight years, he yielded the See to Wilfrid who did much towards repairing the Cathedral Church; but was again banished after writing to the King demanding the restoration of his lost diocese. In 692, Berchtwald of Canterbury held a Council to consider his position and, repudiating the decrees of Theodore, charged his enemies with having resisted the papal decrees for two and twenty years and, by going to Rome, was absolved from all faults by John, who ordered his restoration. The dying Alfric at first refused to recall the sentence; but in the end consented to his reinstatement. As he had no friends in his City, he exchanged the See for that of Hexham and the Abbey of Ripon with St. John of Beverley and died in 709.

The monasteries were filled with learned men and (about 700) Aldhelm of Sherborne translated the Psalter into the vernacular, and did much to induce the Celtic clergy to lay aside their (to him) heretical views. He is also credited with building the most perfectly preserved Saxon church in England (Chad's Church at Bradwell has been disused for many years till recently restored and dedicated to Divine worship), at Bradford.

When, in consequence of wealth, the English monasteries in the North and East were frequently harried by the Danes who went so far inland as Bury, and while Offa remained indifferent so long as Mercia was untouched, the churchmen saw that the conquest of the country by the still heathen Danes would mean injury to the Church, and the Bishops Herefrid of Worcester and Wilbert of Sherborne assisted Edgar of Wessex to defeat them at Hengist's Down (835); and, twelve years later, Ealston of Sherborne was victorious near Glastonbury. In 870, when Edmund refused the offer of Ubba and Ingwar to retain his kingdom if he would abjure Christianity, he was martyred. According to a legend his body was guarded by a wolf till discovered by his friends who buried it in St. Gregory by St. Paul's (1013), whence it was taken to Greenstead and interred in the Abbey of Bury. Bardney and Crowland were sacked and the monks of Lindisfarne, compelled to leave their monasteries, took the body of St. Cuthbert to Melrose and thence to Chester-le-Street, and finally to Durham. The power of these savage invaders was checked by the learned King Alfred, who expressed his regret that but few Englishmen south of Watling street and the Thames could follow the Church Service or even translate Latin into English: and, to restore learning in this country, invited Asser and Grimbald from Wales and the Netherlands and founded many schools. He is said to have translated many passages from the Vulgate, and his laws were modelled on the Decalogue.

Phlegmund of Canterbury (891–918), elected by "the choice of the Church of God and by the folk", aided Edmund the Elder to resist the Danes, and Offa of Mercia granted a tax on each household to maintain an English college in Rome founded by Ina.

Odo of Canterbury (941) had been a soldier and tried to enforce almost military discipline upon the clergy. Down to his time it had been customary for the secular clergy to marry; but he withdrew this liberty from them by transferring cathedral and collegiate churches with their revenues to the monasteries, and thus reducing the canons and parsons to poverty. In this he was aided by Dunstan, a man of noble birth who, disappointed by the coldness of a lady of the court, took regular orders and became Abbot of Glastonbury. A skilful musician, a painter, a jeweller and a blacksmith, he used his talents for the benefit of the Church, and is said to have lived in a cell at Glastonbury, five feet by two, which served as chamber, oratory and workshop. He was a favourite of Edred (946) and was known as a statesman; but fell under the displeasure of Edwy (955) as he opposed his marriage to his cousin Elgiva, whose charms were so great that she made her husband neglect the duties of the court. He expelled the secular clergy from their benefices and, with the exception of Canterbury and Wells, replaced them by monks. He was succeeded by his fifteen years old brother, Edgar (958) who was crowned at Accemannecester (Bath), and translated Dunstan to London, allowing him to retain the emoluments of Glastonbury and Worcester. When he visited the former place he divided his ivory staff in two portions which he laid upon the altar, withdrawing one half and leaving the other to the Church. The chroniclers compared him

D

with Romulus, Cyrus, Alexander and Charlemagne, as he confirmed the monasteries in all their privileges and founded or enlarged the houses at Ely, Abingdon, Mede-hampstead (Peterborough), Thorney (Westminster), Worcester and Winchester. Dunstan gradually relinquished his secular functions, and devoted himself to Church matters.

On the death of Odo (in 959), as Elsine died while crossing the Alps to obtain the pall, and Brihthelm of Wells declined the honour, the final choice fell upon Dunstan who obtained the pall from John XII and continued the work of harassing the secular clergy.

Edgar was succeeded by Edward the Martyr who was assassinated in 972 at the instigation of his stepmother, Elfrida, and Dunstan was compelled to crown Ethelred, an act that so affected him that he died in the following year and was succeeded by two archbishops of whom we know but little—Ethelgar and Sigerie (988–1006).

Relieved of the opposition of Dunstan the Danes continued their invasions of England, sailing up the Thames, the Crouch and the Blackwater, and demanded tribute, which was paid by Ethelred at the suggestion of Sigerie, and resisted by the patriotic Saxons, among whom was Brithnoth, Earl of Essex, slain in the battle of Maldon, who had supported the claims of Edgar, and before setting out, gave his manor of Lawling to the church at Canterbury by a deed that contained these words "and should any one being filled with animosity or malevolence damage any part thereof" he "should partake of the fate of Judas and be gnawn by the infernal cerberus in the swamps of Hell".

The Danes already sacked Canterbury (1011), slew or enslaved nine out of every ten of its inhabitants and captured St. Alphage, a monk of Deerhurst, who had been appointed by Dunstan to Winchester and had succeeded Alfric at Canterbury in 1006. After being imprisoned for eight months, he was slain, and his remains after being buried in St. Paul's were interred with great pomp at Canterbury in 1023.

The fighting between the English and Danes continued and the throne was held by Danish kings, of whom Canute built a minster at Canewdon, in which he placed a priest named Stigand as Chaplain. Going to Rome, he was present at the Sacring of Conrad the Emperor by John XX to whom he confirmed the gift of one penny from every English household to support the English College, and he obtained a reduction in the fees for granting the pall to English primates.

After the defeat at Maldon, Ethelred had sent his wife and two children—Edward and Alfred—to Normandy; and, after the death of Hardicanute, the Witan, wishing to have an English king, sent for the two boys, forgetting that a long residence in a foreign court had made them as much strangers as any of the Danish line.

Edward was elected as king in 1042.

The Court was divided between the Norman and the English factions. The first was led by Leofric, Earl of Mercia, and his son Edwin and Morcar; the second by Godwin, Earl of Wessex and his sons Sweyn, Tostig and Harold, who received the earldom of Somerset and Hereford, of Northumbria and of Norfolk, Suffolk, Essex, Cambridgeshire and Huntingdonshire.

As a governor, Edward was a failure—being more of a churchman than a statesman. He practised great austerity, and while the Leofricssons and Godwinssons were settling their differences, he was praying, building churches, founding monasteries, purchasing relics and appointing abbots and bishops.

He promoted Frenchmen to ecclesiastical posts, made Robert of Jumieges Archbishop of Canterbury, and Ulf Bishop of Dorchester. The latter did naught bishoplike and when he presented himself for confirmation Leo IX, the Pontiff, could scarce restrain himself from breaking his staff across his shoulders on account of his ignorance. At the death of Eadsige (1050), Godwin wished to have an English primate, but Edward obtained the translation of Robert from London, who refused to acknowledge the election of the English Stigand to London, and consecrated the moderate Norman to that See.

When the great Earl returned to England, both Robert and Ulf had to leave the country, and Stigand began his unhappy career. Disliked by the Norman party, he was considered schismatic because he retained the temporalities of his former See—Winchester—and wore the pall left behind by Robert until he obtained one from Benedict X who had been elected contrary to the orders of Hildebrand and was declared to be anti-pope by Nicholas II in 1058.

During the rule of Godwin, William of Normandy visited Edward with a view of being nominated as his heir through the remote relationship of the king's mother, Emma, to the ducal family.

Sailing in the Channel, Harold was shipwrecked off the coast of Ponthieu and became a prisoner of the Count William, who made him swear not to hinder him obtaining the Crown of England. The health of the King failed rapidly and he died soon after the ceremony of consecrating the Abbey at Westminster. His nearest heir was Edgar Atheling (the son of Edmund Ironsides and Agatha, daughter of Henry I of Germany) but, as he had been brought up in the Court of Stephen of Hungary, the Witan chose Harold, who was crowned by Aldred of York as there was a doubt as to the legitimacy of Stigand as primate. Tostig tried to regain his earldom of Northumbria (which had been granted to Edwin, the brother of Morcar Leofricsson) and, aided by Harold Hardrada of Norway, landed in England, to be defeated at Stamford Bridge, September 20, 1066. Three days afterwards, William landed his troops at Pevensey, and Harold made

a forced march to the South. As he passed through
Mercia, Edwin Leofricsson refused to allow him to raise
recruits, and he had to be content with his fatigued
soldiers and the raw recruits he could pick up in his
earldom of East Anglia, Essex and Kent. While his men
spent the night before the battle in resting and feasting,
his spies reported that the Norman camp was full of
priests (being shaven) who were engaged in confessing
and receiving absolution. The battle of Hastings was
fought and lost. After the death of Harold, the Mercian
earls held a meeting in London and, saying they did not
care who was King of England so long as they were earls
of Mercia, offered the Crown to the Atheling, who soon
made peace with William, who was crowned on Christmas
day (1066) by Eldred of York—some saying that they
refused to crown a foreigner and others that William
refused to be crowned by a schismatic. The Archbishop
was confined in Winchester Castle and then sent to
Normandy, where he died.

CHAPTER THREE

THE NORMAN CHURCH

Alteration in the Sees—Langfranc—Stern Rule at Glastonbury—William II
—Ranulf Flambard—Anselm—Warelwast of Exeter—Rahere and St.
Bartholomew's—Difficulty between Canterbury and York—de Corbeuil
—Marriage of Henry I to Matilda—Stephen.

WILLIAM had obtained the aid of Alexander II who had
sent him a ring containing a hair of St. Peter and a
consecrated banner said to have been worked by Matilda,
Countess of Tuscany; but he was disappointed when
the newly-crowned king told his legate that he would
not hold the kingdom won by his armies as a papal fief
and that he would not allow his servants to be excommunicated without his express consent.

The Norman clergy looked with much disdain upon
those of Saxon origin, especially as many of them were
married and did not scruple to defile themselves and
their sacrifices with "things that they called wives".

Besides this, they indulged in pluralities and the Sees
of Elmham, Sherborne and Exeter were held with those
of Dunwich, Ramsey, Crediton and St. Germains.
William moved the Sees from obscure villages as Wells,
Selsey, Dorchester and Lichfield to the large towns of
Bath, Chichester, Lincoln and Coventry; besides uniting
those of Sherborne and Ramsey (with a residence at
Old Sarum) for his nephew Osmund. Seeing it was
necessary to have a primate at Canterbury, he offered
the arch-diocese to the monk Lanfranc who, at first
refused to accept it as he was ignorant of the vernacular.

Going to Rome to obtain the pall, he studied the archives of the Saxon Church, and finding that it had been independent of Rome since the time of Theobald, refrained from paying periodical visits to the tombs of the Apostles. Strict in his government of the Church, he enforced celibacy upon the urban clergy and devoted much time to amending the text of the Vulgate.

While William looked upon the Saxon clergy as a source of disloyalty and rebellion, the Norman clergy despised them as schismatics and sought by fair means and foul to bring both the regular and secular priests to conforming with Rome. To take one instance: William appointed one Thurstan to the abbotcy of Glastonbury. When the monks resisted his efforts to introduce the Latin plainsong instead of the Gregorian church music, he stationed archers in the nave with instructions to shoot at the disobedient members of the choir. Several of them were slain. The King sent him back to Normandy, but he returned after giving William Rufus £500. To prevent the recurrence of such a scene, Osmund compiled a service known as the Rite of Sarum which was adopted by the dioceses of York, Bangor, Lincoln, Hereford and Exeter.

William II (1087) differed much from his father and, instead of showing his consummate State-craft, was a victim of the Norman-Plantagenet fits of anger to which he gave way after the death of Langfranc (1089) and, largely governed by one Ranulph (Ralph) Flambard, who had worked for the Norman ascendancy before the Conquest, and showed the first William how to take advantage of any breach of the feudal law, and seeing that the clerks held their benefices in free alms, and it was uncertain whether they could be forced to serve the king in his wars on the Continent and, paying the first fruits of their livings to the Pope, that they contributed but little to the royal revenue, advised the King to keep the more

important benefices open as long as he could to obtain
their incomes.

"This Ranulph was a poller of the richman and the
undoer of the poore, a confiscator of other men's inheritance, an uncivil lawyer. The king would often laugh at
him and say he was a man which could compasse his
matters as to please his master. He being the Author,
Churches were set for sale, as soon as the Incumbent was
dead—for straight way this Ranulph was sent to take an
inventorie of all that was found and the same to bee
confiscate to the kinges use, and inquirie was made for
one meete to set in the place of the Bishop Abbot or
other deceased, not for their worthinesse, but for their
money that would give most who at length should have
the presentation naked and bare; notwithstanding they
paid dear for it. There was no man rich, but collectors of
money, no clerks but men of lawe not of conscience; no
priests but Farmours. What crime soever any man
committed, so soone as he did appeal for the kinges
advantage by accusing other, he was hearde, yea the
rope was taken from their necks."—ANNALES.

The arch-see remained empty for two years as Anselm
(a monk of Rec) refused to accept it, saying that the
plough of England had been drawn by two oxen (William
and Lanfranc) and, when they were dead, they wished
to yoke a sheep (himself) by the side of an untamable bull
(Rufus), till William forced the primatical staff into his
hands. When compelled to do homage to his temporalities, and when Rufus refused to accept a sum of £500
as his relief he gave that sum to the poor.

Soliciting permission to go to Rome to receive the
pall, the King (Rufus) mockingly asked him to which
Pope he would go—to Gregory VII (1073–1086) residing
at the Vatican or to Guibert, recognised by the imperialists as Clement III. As a way out of the difficulty, a
Council of Bishops sitting at Rockingham advised him

to proclaim the English Church as independent, but he was not strong enough to resist the authority of the Pope although he could disregard that of the King.

William sent envoys to each Pope, seeking to get the best terms from either. When Urban sent Anselm the pall, he, Anselm refused to take it from the legate till the latter laid it upon the altar, whence he took it saying he had received it straight from the hands of St. Peter! When the King wanted money to lend to his brother, Robert, the archbishop offered him a very small sum as a loan from the temporalities. This so enraged the King that Anselm had to flee beyond the seas, and was welcomed by Pascal (1099–1116), who introduced him to a Council sitting at Bari as the "Vicar apostolic and head of the Church of the second world".

William was succeeded by his brother Henry (1100), who claimed to be an Englishman, and made himself popular by granting the "English Charter", promising freedom to the Church and the protection of vacant benefices from spoliation during vacancies, imprisoned Flambard, who escaped from the Tower, and recalled Anselm. He sought popularity by soliciting the hand of Matilda of Scotland (niece of the "Atheling"), but found many difficulties in the way. When her aunt, the abbess Christina, averse to anything that tended to make the Norman line popular, held that such a marriage would be sacrilege, as the princess had taken vows as an initiate, Matilda declared that she had only done so to protect herself from the insults of the Normans, and that twice— when her hand had been sought by the Earls of Richmond and Surrey—she had renounced her vows, and only resumed the regular habit when threatened with blows. Henry consulted Anselm who, fearing to give a personal answer, called together a Synod that declared her to be free from the compulsory observance of vows taken under duress.

The next year, the Archbishop summoned a council of clerics and nobles to find some means of curbing the laxity of morals among the clergy, and six abbots and "many clerks, both French and English, lost their staves and authority, which they acquired unjustly, and were living in iniquity" as having purchased their offices from William and the Bishop, but refused consecration by Anselm, and as Anselm refused to consecrate them the Bishops appointed by the King went to solicit that benefit from Thurstan of York, who refused to interfere in the business of the Southern Province, and Henry had to content himself with levying heavy fines upon those married clergy who clung to their wives. Anarchy showed itself in all ranks of the clergy, and Paschal sent the Archbishop of Vienne to bring about a rule of order, but he was so unpopular that he had to return.

In 1103, when Anselm's messengers returned from Rome with letters repudiating the verbal message that the King might follow the custom of the country brought by the Bishops, he excommunicated the former envoys as being untrue to the Church, and, Henry, jealous of the regal power, demanded that the prelate should perform homage for his temporalities, but he was as obstinate as before, and the King suggested another appeal to Rome in order that Anselm might obtain a concession that would satisfy both. But this was anticipated by Warelwast of Exeter, who took to Rome an instalment of Peter's Pence and declared that Henry would rather give up his crown than abandon his claim to the right of investiture. Anselm, knowing that his life was in danger, refused to return, and excommunicated the King till the latter agreed to leave the election of the bishops in the hands of the chapters assembled in the royal courts, and to receive homage from the temporalities after consecration.

One of Henry's boon companions, a certain Rahere, a minstrel and a jester, was grievously sick at Rome, and had a vision of being taken by a four footed and winged beast to the brink of an abyss at the top of a high hill, where St. Bartholomew directed him to build a hospital to his memory in London. On his return, he found a "marish ground, a common laystall of vordure and filth and a place where felons and other transgressors were executed".

"This Rahere joined unto him a certain old man named Alfune that not long before builded the parish church of St. Giles, nigh to a gate of the citie called Creeples gate; this man he used as a counsellor and companion in his building of the church and hospitall & one of them, to wit Rahere, became the first Prior of that priory, the other, to wit Alfune, became hospitaller and proctor for the poore, and went himself daily to the shambles and other markets, where he begged the charity of devout people for their reliefe promising to liberall givers (alledging testimonies of holy scripture) reward at the hands of God".—Annales.

In 1109 Anselm died, and for five years the revenues of Canterbury found their way into the royal exchequer till Ralph d'Escures (Bishop of Rochester), who had performed many primatical duties, was promoted to the archsee. When Thurstan (successor to Thomas of York) refused to swear canonical obedience to Canterbury, he was denied the benefit of consecration and had to go to France, where he was consecrated at Rheims by the Pope Calistus who gave him independence of Canterbury; but the King forbade him to officiate in any capacity outside the limits of his diocese.

D'Escures was succeeded by William de Corbeuil, whose life was not beyond suspicion, and he is said to have followed the example of Ranulf, having appropriated certain funds belonging to the archsee. Going to Rome for his pall, he came to an understanding with Calistus, who suggested that the dispute between Canterbury and

Rome should be decided by a Council of English bishops presided over by a *legate a latere*. When John de Crema came over for this purpose (although only a deacon), he claimed precedence over bishops and lords, and, on Easter Day, said Mass under a rich canopy, which aroused the wrath of Corbeuil as an infringement of his rights.

After the death of his son, Henry made his nobles swear allegiance to his daughter, Matilda, and his son, Henry; but on his death, many refused to be bound by it, as a woman could not pass on the right she could not enjoy herself.

Stephen of Blois, who posed as next of kin to the Conqueror, gained over the Bishop of Winchester by the promise of succession to Canterbury and those of Salisbury (Chief Justiciar), Ely (Treasurer), and Lincoln, and the citizens of London, and was crowned by Corbeuil in 1138.

This was a miserable time for England. The conflicting nobles, fighting nominally for Stephen or Henry, were really fighting against each other—neighbour against neighbour—but all united against the smaller holders and peasants. We read that they "spared neither church or churchyard, but took all that was valuable therein. Neither did they spare the lands of the bishops, abbots or priests, but robbed the monks and the clergy; and every man plundered his neighbour as much as he could. If three men rode into a town, all fled before them, as though they were robbers. The bishops and clergy were forever cursing them; but this was worth nothing, as they were on all occasions foresworn and reprobate. The earth bore no corn; you might as well have tilled the sea for the land was ruined by foul deeds. And it was openly said that Christ and His Saints were sleeping. "The northern lands from the Ribble and the Tyne were in the hands of Malcolm; Ranulph of Chester was consolidating his lands into an independent principality; the

Duke of Gloucester and the Angevins were masters in the West; de Mandeville and others were devastating the Eastern counties, and Geoffrey was over-running Normandy.

Gilbert à Beket, a landowner and burgess of Rouen, married Rhodesia, daughter of a townsman of Rouen, and, coming to England, became Port Reeve of London. Although he was involved in financial difficulties, he built a chapel in St. Paul's Churchyard. His son, Thomas, was educated at Merton College, and sent to Paris to gain an insight into social and commercial life, and entered into the household of Osbert Huit Deniers and then into that of Archbishop Theobald, who gave (while yet in minor orders) the lucrative Archdeaconry of Canterbury. As agent for the last, he saw how powerless the primate was as compared to the Bishop of Winchester as papal legate. After a quarrel with Foliot of London, he was sent to Rome to oppose the crowning of Stephen's son, Eustace, and attended the Council of Rheims, Auxerre and Boulogne.

As agent for Theobald he invited Henry Fitz Empress to assert his claim to the throne, and obtained his recognition from Stephen on his promising that his second son should retain the earldom of Sussex.

CHAPTER FOUR

BEKET

An English Pope—Beket Chancellor—Quarrel with King—Death of Beket—Geoffrey Plantagenet—College of Canterbury—Penance of Henry—Richard I—Tyranny of Longchamps—Captivity and Release of Richard—Fitz Osbert—St. Hugh—Disputed Succession at Canterbury—Langton—Magna Carta—Gerald of St. David's—His eventful Life—Rich—Feeling Against Alien Clergy—Groslete—Foundation of New Sarum—People Loyal—Boniface—Savoy—Kingdom of Naples.

NICHOLAS BREAKSPEARE was the son of a priest of Esth who, entering a monastery, left his son (born before 1100) to take care of himself. Going to Paris, he entered the house of St. Rufus near Arles and was made cardinal by Eugenius II, who sent him to Norway, where he organised the diocese of Trendheim and obtained the recognition of the archbishop of Vasa as legate, perpetual vicar and primate of Norway and Sweden. On his return to Rome he was elected, as the successor of Anastasius IV, as Adrian IV—the first and the last English Pontiff (1154).

He sent Henry I a copy of the Creed and the Lord's Prayer which may be represented here as a specimen of the English of the period.

PETER: I beleue in God Fader Almichty shipper[1] of heven and earth.

ANDREW: And in Jhesu Christ His onelethe Son ure Louerde.

[1] Maker.

JAMES: This is iuange thruch the Holy Gost, bore Mary
    Maiden:

JOHN: Tholed pine[1] under Pounce Pilat; picht on Rode,[2]
    dede and yburiid;

THOMAS: Licht into Helle; the thridde say from death
    a rose;

JAMES ALPHAEUS: Steich[3] into Heven; sit on His Fader
    richt honde; God Almichty;

PHILIP: Then is comende to deme[4] the quik and the
    dede;

BARTHOLOMEW: I beleue in the Holy Gost;

MATTHEW: All Holie Churche;

SIMON: Home of al holnes; forgivenis of sin;

THADDEUS: Flies[5] vprising;

MATTHIAS: Lif withuten ende.

                      Amen.

Ure Fadir in hevene riche
Thi name be haliid eueriliche
Thou bring us to thi michilblisse
Thi will to wirke thu us wille
Als hit is in hevene ido
Euer in earth ben hit also
That holi bred that lasteth ay.
Thou send hit ous this ilke day
Forgiue ous all that we havith don
As we forgiueth uch other mon
He let us falle in no founding
Ak scilde us fro al foule thing.

              —ANNALES.

From Typographise Hiberniae from Giraldus Cambrensis.

Henry II (1100) was determined to restore the royal
power wasted by the years of anarchy and civil war,

[1] Suffered.   [3] Rose.
[2] Was crucified.   [4] Judge.
      [5] Body.

and would have done much to redeem England had he not spoilt all by his, the proverbial, ungovernable temper of the Angevin kings that led him into serious conflicts with the Church.

Not only King of England, he had rights over Scotland and Wales, was by inheritance Lord of Normandy and Maine and by his marriage with Eleanor of Anjou of Guinne, Poitou, Langue d'Oc, Auvergne Perigord, Angouleme, Gascony and the Limousin—owning more territory in France than the King himself.

Recognising the ability of Beket, Henry made him Chancellor, little dreaming that the gay courtier's boon companion was in reality a man of austerity and wore beneath his gay attire a hair shirt; but, he did his work well, being a good administrator, replacing the base coinage by a good currency, slighting the castles of the turbulent nobles and causing them to dismiss their mercenary soldiers. The Church was in a bad state and the clergy shielded themselves behind their "benefit". The King thought that he saw in his Chancellor a means of curbing their arrogance and licentiousness and on the death of Theobald nominated him (as yet but a deacon) to the Primacy. Hastily ordained as a priest, he was eight days later consecrated to Canterbury by thirteen bishops. Before he had enjoyed that office twelve months, he successfully contested the levying of the Sheriff's and (the land tax) upon Church lands, demanded the surrender of certain benefices then in the King's hands and the restoration of the castles at Rochester, Saltwood and Hythe and the manor of Tonbridge (which had been confirmed by several bishops to the Earl of Gloucester) to Canterbury. On the other hand, Henry demanded Beket's resignation of various benefices he held *in commendam* and the quarrel thus commenced lasted till his death.

The struggle became more and more acute. Clerks (in major and minor orders) claimed the right of being tried in Church courts which could only inflict terms of imprisonment and fines and generally contented themselves with unfrocking the culprit. Henry was determined that this should cease and that, when unfrocked, he should be handed over to the secular power for punishment. Holding a Council at Clarendon, he demanded that all clerks accused of offences should be tried in the royal courts, and that a royal justice should be present at all Church courts; that laymen should be represented by Counsel in ecclesiastical courts; that appeals from church courts should be from the bishop to the king, and that, on a vacancy in dioceses, abbeys and priories of royal foundation, the revenues should revert to the exchequer and the chapters should assemble in the chapel royal to elect (with the King's consent) a successor who, before his consecration, should do homage for his temporalities "saving his order".

Beket expressed his willingness to withdraw his favourite phrase, "Saving my order", and the King said that he was willing to act towards the Archbishop as "the lowliest of his predecessors had acted towards the weakest of his".

But this partial reconciliation was frustrated by the crowning of the young King, Henry, by the Archbishop of York, and Henry exclaimed in his anger that among his courtiers he had not one who would avenge the insult he had received from the Archbishop and relieve him of this low born priest.

Although Beket offered the King 20,000 marks to be allowed to surrender the primacy, it was refused, and he went to Rome where he told Paschal III that he had not been canonically elected but had been thrust upon the Church by a layman, and, at the same time, surrendering the Staff and Ring to him, received them back from him the next day (thus making him hold his office from the Holy See) and ordered his legate to

E

repudiate the Constitutions of Clarendon under pain of interdict. Henry then appealed to Guy de Crema, declared by the Emperor to be Pope in succession to the Anti-Pope Victor.

Four knights—le Breton, Fitzurse, de Morville and de Tracy—rode post haste to Canterbury and forced their way into the presence of Beket who, knowing their errand, fled into the Cathedral where he was slain. The King was terrified at the result of his words and saw—too late—that he had lost a friend who would—if properly treated—have served his end in building up a powerful government.

It was difficult to bring the murderers to justice as Beket had declared that all offences against churchmen should be tried in the Church courts. The Bishop of Exeter wrote to the Pope demanding that they should be tried as enemies to the Church; but nothing was done. Geoffrey Riddel, John of Oxford and Richard of Ilchester were promoted to the Archdeaconry of Poitiers and the Sees of Norwich and Ely and Henry agreed with Paschal that anyone who murdered a cleric should be tried by the chief justiciar in the presence of a bishop.

Prince Henry ordered the Prior of Canterbury to proceed to the election of an archbishop. Roger of Bec declined that honour and then the choice fell upon Richard (prior of Dover), who was not agreeable to the Prince and had to go to Rome to be consecrated and granted the use of the pall. Roger of York refused to appear before a synod in London as he was not allowed to have his cross borne before him within the Sees of Lincoln, Lichfield (Chester), Worcester and Hereford which are in the Southern Province. The clergy of York demanded satisfaction for the excommunication of the clergy of St. Oswald for not acknowledging his election, and those of St. Asaph the restoration of their bishop who had resigned his See from which he had been driven by the Welsh on being appointed guardian of the vacant Abbey of Abingdon; but, as the King appointed a new abbot, he lost both See and Abbey. This synod condemned the libertinage and simony among the clergy, has provided a better method of administrating the Eucharist and prohibited private marriages, especially between minors.

In the following year, another one made an attempt to induce the prelates of the Scots Church to acknowledge the supremacy of that of England.

Geoffrey, the natural son of the king, had been appointed to the See of Lincoln; but, as he neglected to seek consecration of five years, he was ordered by the Pope to be consecrated or resign. He did the latter, and gave the charge into the hands of Richard.

Owing to a dispute with the monks of St. Augustine, who claimed to be free from episcopal jurisdiction, Richard (1176) ordered them to produce their charters, some of which he denounced as forgeries. In order to lessen their influence, he planned the erection of a college of secular canons in Canterbury, which was opposed by the monks, as it might deprive them of the right to elect the archbishop and, when they sent a representative to Rome, he deprived them of their functions, and the project dropped for a time. On his death (1185) the chief justiciar ordered the monks to hold an election, and Baldwin (who held the See till 1193) was elected.

Henry was sore beset by domestic troubles. Eleanor had induced his sons, with the assistance of Louis of France, William of Scotland, and the Count of Flanders, to rebel against him while the Norman barons were preparing for an invasion of East Anglia, where Bigot was already in arms against him. He then remembered that the murder of Beket had been committed with his connivance and, returning to England (1174), rode post haste to Canterbury, dismounted and walked barefooted from St. Dunstan's Church to the Cathedral where he prostrated himself before the tomb of the Martyr and spent the night in watching, fasting and praying, having ordered the monks to scourge him in expiation of the crime. While still in the city, he visited the shrine in the company of Louis of France who gave to the memory of the saint a rich cup set with precious stones and a large single stone called the Regal (either a diamond or a carbuncle) which remained at Canterbury till the Dissolution, when it was made into a ring for Henry. The last we hear of it is when it formed part of a necklace worn by Mary I.

Baldwin thought that the secular priests would be more amenable to the royal pleasure than the regular orders and planned the erection of a college of canons in Canterbury, and, when the monks sent a protest to Rome, he forced an unpopular prior upon them and suspended them from their functions. Although Henry begged him to desist, he persevered and commenced to build a college near St. Dunstan's Church.

Henry closed his turbulent life in 1189, and was succeeded by his eldest son, Richard, who inherited Normandy, Anjou, Touraine, Guienne and Poitou; Geoffrey being well provided for in the duchy of Brittany, and John being lord of Ireland.

Richard spent but a small portion of his ten years' reign (1189–1199) in England, which he looked upon as a milch cow to supply the costs of his futile wars in France and Palestine.

Geoffrey Riddel of Ely had died in the time of Henry, who seized upon his estate on the plea of intestacy. At a Synod held at Pipewell, Geoffrey Plantagenet, Chancellor Longchamps, de Lucy, Richard of Ely and Walter, Dean of York, were appointed to York, Ely, Winchester, London and Salisbury. The Bishops of Salisbury and Durham protested against the translation of Geoffrey as they were not present; and Walter, because he had been guilty of bloodshed in putting down rebellions against his father.

Richard then raised money by selling offices, including the life interest in the earldom of Northumberland and the perpetual succession to the earldom of Sedbury to Hugh of Durham.

Longchamps acted with great severity, arresting his colleague of Durham whom he deprived of the earldom and the custody of the castles of Newcastle-on-Tyne and Windsor, deprived the clergy and laity of their churches, kept churches and abbeys vacant for his own profit and that of his creatures and travelled about the country with fifteen hundred horsemen and such a retinue of knights, minstrels and servants that many of the convents at which he stayed spent a whole year's revenue upon their entertainment.

As the mutual jealousies of the Christian princes in the Holy Land showed Richard that the Crusades would end in Civil strife, he left in the guise of a travelling merchant. Being shipwrecked in the Adriatic, he was captured by the Duke of Austria who transferred him to the Emperor on the payment of £60,000 which, when it came to a question of ransom, was raised to £100,000.

John then immediately paid homage to the French King for the Continental possessions; but Eleanor, anxious to retain the Angevin dominions intact, set to work to raise the necessary amount, and so great was the enthusiasm for Richard (or hatred of John) that the clergy granted one tenth of their tythes and the bishops, abbots and nobles one quarter of their incomes, the Cistercians one year's sale of their wool, and the parishes melted down their chalices and plate to the amount of £20,000 on condition that the sums advanced were to be repaid within one year of the King's return.

This effort weighed heavily upon the poorer taxpayers, especially in the city of London, where the members of the wealthiest guilds claimed the right of sitting upon the aldermanic bench and assessing themselves. A certain William Fitz Osbert, of Norman descent, proclaimed himself the champion of the poor with such success that Stow says that he had "52,000 Londoners at his devotion". Like many demagogues, he freely quoted Scripture, and told the poor men that they "long essayed the hard hand of ye rich men", and stated that he was the "Saviour of ye poore men", exhorted them to "draw wholesome water foorth of my welles and that with joy for the day of youre visitation is at hand. I will separate the people humble and meek and full of good faith from the proud and faithless. I will part the chosen from the reprobate and light from darkness". Going to see Richard when in France, he was repulsed and, returning, had to take shelter in the church of St. Mary le Bow, whence he was smoked out and hanged at Smithfield, forsaking "Mary's Son and calling upon the devil to help him".

In order to expiate the death of Beket, Henry built the Carthusian priory of Witham in Somerset on which he placed Hugh d'Avinal, afterwards Bishop of Lincoln (1186).

A strict disciplinarian in many respects, he was lax in enforcing celibacy upon the clergy; he hated pomp, superstition and relic-mongering, and had great influence over both Henry and Richard, being able to refuse to install a courtier recommended by the first as a canon in his cathedral saying that preferments were meant for churchmen and not for royal favourites, and did not hesitate to excommunicate a royal forester without consulting the King as, he said, he knew the latter would approve of his action.

When the King demanded a heavy subsidy, he said that

the homage performed for the temporalities did not render the clergy liable for service in continental wars, and the officer sent to confiscate his goods refused to obey for fear of anathema.

Travelling to France to intercede with Richard on behalf of his colleagues, he was met at Rouen by some nobles who begged him to return, lest he should meet with bodily harm as the King was attending Mass; but, he boldly advanced and forced the King to give him the kiss of peace. "If all bishops", said Richard, "were like Hugh, no king could withstand them". On his death in 1200, his funeral was attended by two kings, three archbishops, fourteen bishops, a hundred abbots and many nobles. He was canonised twenty years later.

Although Geoffrey had enjoyed the temporalities of the See, Baldwin refused to consecrate him to York, and he had to go to Rome, where Celestine confirmed his election granted him the pall, and exempted his See from all jurisdiction save that of the legate. When he arrived at Dover, he was arrested, and, after seeking sanctuary in St. Martin's Church, was dragged from the altar and imprisoned.

On the death of Baldwin, the monks elected Robert Fitzwalter as his successor. He was "a man of incomparable understanding, a singular pillar of stability and of great wisdom," who was able to keep John (1199) within bounds by restraining his fits of terrible wrath (common to the Norman and Plantagenet lines) while he lived. On his death in 1207, the King offended both the English and Norman nobility by repudiating his wife (Hawisa of Gloucester) to marry Isabella, the affianced bride of the powerful Earl of Marche.

The Church was in a critical state, both morally and financially, and the King kept the Sees vacant as long as possible in order to divert the proceeds of the temporalities into the royal exchequer. The Civil government

was in no better state, as the exactions of the King goaded
the barons into silent rebellion. The Papal Chair was
then occupied by Innocent III (1198), who proved to be
a strong pontiff and now had an opportunity to interfere
with the English Church, since, on the death of Fitzwalter, the younger monks of Canterbury elected their
sub-prior, Reginald, to the Primacy and John selected
de Grey (of York) for that office. The first was sent to
Rome to obtain the pall, and, although the monks
enjoined upon him an obligation of secrecy, no sooner
had he crossed the Channel than he let everybody know
his errand.

Innocent refused to acknowledge either the first,
because he had been appointed by a layman, and the
second because of his ignorance, and recommended
Stephen Langton who, although a doctor and rector of
the Paris University, was a thorough Englishman and
opposed to all papal pretensions. When he was accepted
by the monks, the King sent men at arms to Canterbury,
confiscated the possessions of the Abbey and many of
the monks had to flee across the sea for personal safety.
This arbitrary act caused Innocent to excommunicate
the King and place an interdict upon the realm by which
the churches, save those of the Templars and Hospitallers,
were closed except for the purpose of baptisms and
burials, lest souls be imperilled and public health endan-
gered. The Bishop of London not only refused to publish
these dread letters, but encouraged their clergy to do the
same.

Langton and Marychurch (of London) went to Rome
to make the miserable state of the country known to
the Pope, who declared John to be deposed and
entrusted Philippe of France with the task of
depossessing him.

When John was ready to invade France with 60,000
men, he met the legate, Pandulph, at Dover and delivered

to him his orb and sceptre which were retained for some days and returned on his agreeing to hold England and Ireland as papal fiefs on the payment of £600 to £700 a year. This was confirmed by some of the barons and bishops on the promise that Langton and other exiled prelates should be allowed to return with safety and life and limb, and granted £8,000 for the payment of their debts and cost of returning. Under date of 1245, we read that in the great fire in the Wardrobe "the dishonourable Charter which John made was burned".— ANNALES.

In his difficulty John took the vow of a Crusader and made a five years' truce with Philippe. Langton held a Synod at Dunstable where the legate Nicholas was accused of withholding the great part of the Peter Pence.

The Barons took up arms, being led by Lord Fitzwalter, who raised the Standard of the "Army of God and of the Church" and compelled the King to sign the Great Charter of 1215; but, scarcely was the ink dry than he again exiled Langton and forbade him to return till he had paid a heavy fine. The King then harried the lands of the Bishops of London, Winchester, Bath and Wells, Lincoln, Worcester, Coventry and Rochester for having forced him to sign that Charter, by which the liberties of the Church as regards elections, taxation of the spiritualities on presentation, were assured.

John lost his crown whilst crossing the Wash, and died at Newark in 1216, being succeeded by his infant son, Henry III, under the care of the Earl of Pembroke, Peter des Roches of Winchester, and the legate Guale, as representing the English and Norman barons and the Church.

A striking ecclesiastical character of this period was Gerald, Bishop of St. David's, more familiarly known as Giraldus Cambrensis. He was the grandson of the beautiful Nesta—the mistress of Henry II—and, in 1171, was elected Bishop of St. David's, in which capacity he claimed jurisdiction over the Sees of Llandaff, Bangor, St. Asaph, Hereford and Worcester and refused to acknowledge the primacy of Canterbury. Henry, who had declared that no Welshman should hold a Welsh See, summoned the Chapter to Winchester, confiscated their wealth and ordered them to elect Peter de Leia, who went to his diocese with a large retinue to whom he made large grants of land and imposed a heavy taxation upon the priests, payable at the festivals of the Church. He was driven out after eight years.

In the meantime, Gerald had fled to France, whence he had to return, as the King did not wish him to embroil himself with him of England on account of an obscure priest. He then refused the offer of an archbishopric and four bishoprics in Ireland, as he knew he should be rejected as a foreigner. Returning to Wales, he was spared personal illtreatment on account of his powerful relations, and de Leia appointed him as his deputy till his death, when he was re-elected.

John declared this election void and Baldwin, who was seeking to extend the authority of Canterbury over the principality, refused to allow him to be consecrated. Going to Rome to justify his position, he could only produce some time-worn parchments while the King sent Foliot of London (accompanied by four canons of St. David's, who bore witness against the independence of the See) with handsome presents to the Curia. In 1194, Baldwin had invaded Wales under the pretext of raising forces for the Crusades, confiscated his effects and declared that all who gave food or shelter were traitors.

He was one of the most accomplished scholars of his age, combining an excellent writer to the stately diction of Latin composition with the humour of a minstrel, as well as being a troublesome bishop. It was not till the time of Archbishop Peckham (1220) that the Welsh Church became subject to Canterbury.

We will now glance at two remarkable ecclesiastics. Edmund Rich (1207–1245) like many great churchmen was born in humble circumstances. Studying at Abingdon and Paris, he returned to England and threw himself into the pursuit of knowledge as taught by the Friars, and distinguished himself by his lectures. At first he was an ardent curialist till the study of the Vulgate and the Decretals caused him to doubt the doctrine of papal supremacy. When elected to the Southern primacy (1234) he called a council of prelates to insist upon the observance of the charters.

When Englishmen complained that the Pope provided aliens to English benefices who farmed them at a high rate to curates to the neglect of the services and religious teaching and the dilapidation of the fabrics, and of the cost, in time and money, caused by the appeals to Rome, the Pope replied that the cardinals, upon whom depended the government of the Church, were prevented from receiving prebends in cathedral churches; that nuncios had to sue for royal permission to carry out their missions, and were even imprisoned, and that magistrates refused to imprison excommunicated persons who remained impenitent for forty days.

While the laymen refused to pay the tenth of their income towards papal exactions, those clerks who had obtained their benefices through provision were less able to refuse. Certain malcontents (led by Sir Robert Twenge) not only sent threatening letters to the alien priests, but went about disguised in visards, spreading terror into their hearts by burning their houses and barns. The legate himself was captured at St. Albans, and only released on paying a large ransom.

Rich had not the staying power of Langton, or, perhaps he found it more difficult to resist the Spiritual than the temporal authority, and he died abroad in 1245.

Stow thus speaks of this great man, whose death was hailed with delight by the curialists—"An Englishman born in Suffolk, whose learning in Hebrew, Greek, in Latin and other languages, won for him perpetual consideration; hee was the manifeste blamer of pope and king; a reprover of prelates; a corrector of monks; a director of clerkes; a sustainer of scholars; a preacher of the people; a persecutor of unchaste livers; a diligent searcher of the Scriptures; a mallet to such strangers as sought preferment in the Realm by ye popes provisions; In housekeeping—liberall, in corporal refection—plentiful and in administering spiritual foode—devoute and godly affectionate; in his Bishop's office diligent, reverend and never weary. He gave his bookes to the Fryers Minors in Oxford."—ANNALES.

Robert Grostete of Lincoln was a stronger man and ruled his extensive diocese of Lincoln in a satisfactory manner from 1234 to 1253. Fearless in his attempts to do justice to all without respect of persons, he utilised the religious enthusiasm of the Friars, and insisted upon religious houses making due provision for the services in impoverished parishes. Like many churchmen, he fell away from subservience to the Curia when he realised the pride of the foreign clergy, joined the patriotic or national party and restrained abuses with a strong hand. When the king would have given the See of Chichester to a court favourite, he succeeded in obtaining it for his nominee—Richard de la Wyche—and defended his action in refusing to install a youthful papal candidate in a canonry in his cathedral on the ground that such presentations robbed Christians of the administrations of their proper pastors and were opposed to the sanctity of the Holy See and the Christian and Catholic Church, and did not hesitate when preaching before Innocent and his cardinals at the Council of Lyons (1250) to trace the source and origin of all the evils in the Church to "entrusting the care of the flocks to ravening wolves licensed by the Court of Rome ".

It was about this time that the cathedral of Salisbury was erected. Most of the larger churches were built by many men during the course of centuries, but this majestic pile only took thirty-eight years to complete during the lives of two bishops.

We have already seen how the Sees of Wilton and Sherborne were united to form that of Old Sarum in 1075 for the benefit of Osmund. As the cathedral was within the king's town, the disputes between the ecclesiastical and military authorities gave rise to continual brawls between the canons of the church and the soldiers of the castle. During a Rogation week procession, the soldiers got between the clergy and the town and so molested the latter that they kept within their precincts for the rest of the year. The Bishop—Herbert le Poor (died 1217)—was unable, through lack of funds, to remove the cathedral, but his brother—Richard (who succeeded him)—obtained, by the help of the legate Gualo, the necessary permission from Pope Honorius and, persuading the canons to set apart a portion of their prebends to defray the cost, purchased Merryfields (St. Mary's field) as the future site, where, in 1220, he performed Divine Service in a small wooden chapel, and, taking off his shoes, proceeded to the site of the new church, chanting the Litany; he laid three stones—for Honorius, for Boniface and for himself; after which William Longspee of Salisbury and his countess, Elai de Vitre, laid two more.

The Bishop and Canons then took up their abode in New Sarum and were followed by the citizens "fearing to lose their bellie cheer (for they were wont to have

banketting at every station, a thing commonly practised
by the religious of old, who wished to link in the commons
unto them) whom any man may lead whither he will
by the bellie"; or as Latimer said, "with beefe and
beere". In 1225, the bishop, with the help of the archbishops of Canterbury and Dublin, consecrated three
altars and, the day after the feast of St. Michael, the
bishop preached in the new building.

In 1237, the legate, Otto, held a great council in St.
Paul's, nominally to arrange for a visitation of the
monasteries but, in reality, to prevent clerks holding
benefices in plurality which would thus provide more for
the aliens. At this council, canons still in force were
passed—allowing laymen under certain circumstances to
administer the rite of baptism, and forbidding the
alienation of tythes, the holding of benefices in plurality
or in commendam without a license, the commutation
of penance for monetary considerations and the receipt of
money for administering the Sacraments.

When Otto left England he was only regretted by those
who looked to him for preferment and the king. Stow
describes Henry III as one "who permitted all things,
he breaketh promises, faith and law in all points and hath
married a stranger without the consent or knowledge of
his friends or natural subjects and now secretly called in
ye legate, it is now sayd that Edmund, Archbishop of
Canterbury did blame the king especiall for calling in
the legate whereby he knew that great prejudice would
ensue, to the great detriment of the Realm, but the king
not regarding the Archbishop's counsell or anie of his
subjects, would not call back what he had intended".—
ANNALES.

Another legate—Martin—eluded the vigilance of the
government and travelled about the country, demanding
first fruits of the clergy; but the hatred to foreigners was
so great that when one was installed as a Canon in St.

Paul's he was slain, and his murderer was never discovered.

The marriage of Henry with Eleanor of Provence brought many foreigners to England. Among these were Peter and Boniface of Savoy. The first, originally intended for the Church, was a canon of Geneva but soon threw off the cassock, married the heiress of the Faucigny and, coming to England, was made Earl of Richmond; after building the palace known by his name, he returned to his own country and persecuted the citizens of Geneva.

His brother, Boniface, became Archbishop of Canterbury in 1245. At first he seemed inclined to carry out reforms, but soon the pride of race appeared and he treated those whom he thought were his equals with contempt and those who were in subordinate positions with insolence. As Archbishop he spent much of his time abroad and, when at home, invaded the dioceses of his suffragans and infringed the rights of the monasteries. We read in Stow: "In his visitation he came to the pryorie of Saint Bartholomew in Smithfield, where being received with procession in most solemn wise, hee passed not upon the honour, but came to visite them; unto whome the Chanons answered that they, having learned Byshope. ought not in contempt of him be visited by any other, which answere so much misliked the Archbishoppe that he forthwith fell upon the Subpryor and smote him in the face with his fist saying. 'Indeede, indeede, doth it become you English traytors to so answere me?' Thus raging with othes not to be recited, he rent in pieces the rich cope of the Subpryor, trode it under feete. and thrust him against a pillar of the chancell, so he hadde almost killed him. but the Chanons seeing, that their subpryor was almost dead, they ranne and plucked off the Archbyshoppe with such violence, that they overthrew him backwardes, whereby they might see, that he was armed and prepared to fight. The Archbishoppe's men, seeing their maister downe (being all strangers and their master's countrymen borne in Provence) fell upon the Canons and beat them, tare them and trode them under their feete; so at length the Chanons getting away as well as they could ranne bloudie and myrie, rent and torne, to the Bishoppe of London, to complaine, who badde them go to the king at Westminster and telle him thereof; whereupon foure of them went thither. the rest were not able they were so sore hurt, but when they came to Westminster, the king would neither heare them nor see them. so they returned without redresse. In the same season the whole citie was in an uproar and ready to have rung the common bell, and to have hewed the Archbyshoppe in small pieces, but he was gotten away to Lambeth ".—ANNALES.

Innocent III had excommunicated the Emperor Frederic and on his death waged war against his sons Conrad and Manfred to gain possession of Naples, the crown of which he offered to the King of the Romans (Richard of Cornwall) who, seeking the imperial crown, declined it. It was then offered to Henry's younger son Edmund the Crouchback—through the Bishop of Boulogne who absolved Henry of his vow as a Crusader. The King unable to carry on the war, left it to Innocent, who raised money from Italian and Jewish merchants at an exorbitant sale of interest, pledging the land of the exempted monasteries. Thus we read:

"Peter de Eglebank bishoppe of Hereford, in the court of Rome feigning himself Procurator of the cleargie of England, bound the small houses of Religion in one hundred or two hundred marks the piece. St. Edmundsbury was bound in seven hundred marks to be paid to certaine merchant strangers. In all this money was collected to expulse Manfrede out of Naples, Apulia and

Sicill, which the pope had given to Edmund, son of king Henry of England."—ANNALES.

The bad government and extravagance of the Court made the barons rebel under Simon de Montfort and Henry died a defeated king in 1272 at the age of sixty years, after a reign of fifty-six years.

F

CHAPTER FIVE

MORTMAIN, PROVISORS AND PRAEMUNIRE

Papal Exactions—Archbishops—Friar Peckham—Praemunire Condemned at Reading—Decree of Boniface VIII—Babylonian Captivity—Taxation of Clergy—Schism—Winchelsey—Anti-papal Legislation—Edward II—Council of Peers—Reynolds and Bishop—Bull of Clement V— Flight of King—Orleton on Opposition—Edward II—Edward III— War with France—Stratford at Canterbury—Alien Priories—Quarrel between King and Stratford—Islip at Canterbury—Black Death— Ignorance of Clergy—Provision and Indulgences—Papal Review of England—Clerks and Secular Employment—William of Wykeham— Pluralities—Scholars at Oxford.

ON the death of Henry III, Edward I was recovering from wounds received in the Holy Land and Sicily. He returned by slow stages and the government was carried on by Geoffrey of York.

The reigns of the three Edwards are particularly interesting as they show the constant struggle between the Papacy and the Crown, and the Crown with the Barons, the successes of whom varied according to the skill of the Pontiff, the character and needs of the king and the strength of the nobles. The first was claiming universal dominion in matters temporal as well as spiritual and the Church demanded the rights of presentation to all benefices vacant on death or promotion by means of provision and also that of nominating foreigners and cardinals who, being free from episcopal jurisdiction and obligation of residence, here, allow them to farm out their benefices to ill-paid vicars, thus depriving the parishes of religious instruction and hospitality and causing many of the churches and parsonages to fall into decay, while the collectors of the first fruits, Annates and Peter's Pence, sent every year a sum exceeding the royal revenue to defray the expenses of the Pontifical court and papal wars.

On the death of Boniface in 1272, the Canterbury monks elected William Cluttenden who, going to Rome, was convinced of his unfitness, and Innocent VI appointed Robert Kilwarby who, being made Cardinal Bishop of Porto, only held the primacy for one year.

The monks then elected Robert Burnell, but, as he was not acceptable to the Pope, they held a third election and chose the Franciscan, John Peckham, a man of great austerity, and a strong disciplinarian.

The continual alienation of land to the Church by gifts, vows and bequests, which converting it into tenure by free alms, made it exempt from all payment in cases of vacancy by resignation, promotion or death. To remedy this, Parliament passed the Act of Mortmain (1279) prohibiting such gifts without the King's license, and Peckham assembled a Council at Reading at which, not only this measure was strongly condemned, but complaints were made that the Civil authority neglected to imprison those who remain impenitent for forty days after excommunication.

As this meeting was declared to have been illegally called without the royal warrant, Peckham retaliated by ordering the articles of Magna Carta, relating to the liberties of the Church, to be affixed to the church doors, and the clergy to preach against all who should curtail them. When the clerical and lay Parliaments met at York and Northampton, the former made promises and the latter granted a thirteenth.

In 1281 when the dignitaries of the Church refused to grant the payment of one half of the Spiritualities, as the parochial clergy were not represented, and, when the King ordered them to send two representatives from each diocese and chapter to Parliament to vote supplies for the honour of the Church, the peace of the nation and the comfort of the King, Burnell (then Chancellor) questioned the advisability of doing so, as they had full power of taxation in Convocation.

On the death of Peckham, in 1292, two years elapsed before Robert of Winchelsey was elected to succeed him in 1294.

Boniface VIII (1299), elected to the papacy on the resignation of the Minorite Celestine V, offended the King of France by forbidding the clergy to pay taxes levied by the temporal authorities without his permission. His successor, Clement V (1303)—a Frenchman—commenced the Babylonian Captivity by taking up his residence at Avignon and complained to Edward that cardinals, ordained by God to govern the Church, were not allowed to enjoy prebends in English cathedrals; that papal nominees were prevented from taking up English benefices, and that English men were prohibited from carrying appeals to the Court of Rome: that papal nuncios were unable to fulfil their duties till licensed by the King and had even been imprisoned till they paid heavy ransoms.

When Winchelsey knew that Edward intended to tax the clergy, he obtained a bull prohibiting them paying such impositions, and the King summoned the wealthier clergy to grant him an aid payable by all; but when it was pointed out that they had no authority to do so, Convocation granted money for the honour of the Church, the peace of the realm and the comfort of the King.

On the death of the Maid of Norway, there were two claimants for the Scots crown—Robert Bruce and Edward Balliol—and a third in the person of Edward, whose claim was that Balliol was his vassal for the lordship of Cumberland.

Boniface, claiming to be the bestower of all earthly crowns, forbade Edward to intervene till he had given his decision, but Parliament declared that it was against the laws of the realm for English kings to plead their cause before foreign potentates and when Winchelsey warned the King not to proceed in the matter as Jerusalem would not fail to protect her children, or Sion to cherish the Church, he replied that neither Jerusalem or Sion would prevent him from maintaining what everybody knew to be his right. The Bishops supported their Primate who went so far as to affix his official seal to a document treating of the deposition of Edward. When he sought permission to go abroad he was granted a passport for the outward journey but was told that he might need one to return. Benedict deprived him of his episcopal and legatine authority, the monks of Canterbury were severely punished, and the Bishop of Winchester was fined £1,000 for administering to his necessities.

To prevent the cells of the alien monasteries sending money to help his enemies, the King confiscated their possessions, allowing each monk eightpence a week.

During this reign, an important Ecclesiastical law—de Asportatis Religiosorum—prevented the heads of the great religious orders on the Continent coming to England to exact contributions to the parent house; and the Parliament sitting at Carlisle (1307) complained that the richest benefices were given to foreigners (often non-resident) by way of Provision to the prejudice and disherison of founders, benefactors and owners of advowsons; that the revenues of religious houses were granted to cardinals; that first-fruits were rigorously exacted; that Peter's Pence had been trebled; that legacies left for pious purposes were alienated to other objects, and that debts were illegally collected to the prejudice of the Crown. The legal Testa pleaded the authority of the Pope, but was condemned to lodge all moneys then collected with the Parliament, pending their disposal by the King, who, being engaged in war with Scotland and France was obliged to be great friends with the Pope and granted protection to him and his colleague Alameni; but the people refused to pay any further sums to them.

Edward II (1307-1327) was a man of a far different character to his father, and the glory of the reign of Edward I was tarnished during his twenty years' reign. He was swayed by a certain Piers Gaveston, whom he made Earl of Cornwall (a title hitherto confined to the royal family) and to whom he gave his sister (Margaret of Gloucester) in marriage. When the King went to France to marry the Princess Isabelle, he was made regent and entrusted with the granting of *congé d'élire* to the cathedral churches, the taking of the oaths from the bishops, the restoration of their temporalities, the appointments to prebends and other benefices and the rights of wardships. The position he held in the Council offended the nobility, who were led by Thomas, Earl of Lancaster, Leicester and Derby, Lord High Steward of England, heir to the earldom of Ferrers and claimant (through his wife) to that of Lincoln.

Burdened with debts, the King called a Parliament to meet at Westminster where, contrary to the royal instructions, the barons appeared with their retainers fully armed, and placed the government in the hands of Commissioners, who were selected on a plan recalling the oligarchies of Venice and Berne. The Earl selected two bishops and the Bishops two earls; these four selected two barons and these six selected fifteen others: all twenty-one being sworn to make such ordinances as should tend to the honour and advantage of the Church, King and People. When Gaveston failed to suppress the rebellion in Ireland, he was hanged and the King relied upon the advice of the de le Spencers, who obtained the necessary supplies provided the sums were collected by clerical assessors and the freedom of the Church was maintained.

Winchelsey was recalled and he renewed the conflict with the Archbishop of York and opposed the King in his wish to rescind the constitutions of Peckham against pluralities in favour of a court chaplain.

On his death (1313) the monks of Canterbury elected the dean of Salisbury (Cobham) to take his place: but, as he was not a *persona grata* to the King and the Pope, they chose Walter Reynolds who purchased a bull from Clement V (1313) giving him power to visit the diocese of his suffragans and to suspend their functions during such visitations; to grant dispensations to a hundred clerks under canonical age to hold benefices; to absolve a similar number of laymen for having used violence towards clerics and to depose of all cathedral benefits that should fall vacant during his visitations. Before this could be ratified, Clement died and his successor (John XXII) would only confirm it on being promised the nomination of eighteen bishops during the following seventeen years. The clergy were gratified by the passing of the Act of Articuli Cleri (1326) by which they obtained relief in respect to the interference of the lay courts in matters of Church, probates and divorces, maintenance of royal carriages and the exemption of royal mills from tythes; leave of absence for those clerks attending the King's Court; the protection of benefices from waste during vacancies; the admission of clerics to free chapels by laymen; the trial of clerks in lay courts and the relegation of cases relating to bigamy, bastardy, usury, simony, mortuaries, violence towards clerks and offences against churchyards to the Church Courts and complained that informers against the clergy (when acquitted by the law courts) remain unpunished; that clerks were prevented from pleading their benefit of clergy; that persons seeking sanctuary were cut off from provisions; that bishops had ceased to be surety for clerks and that the Act of Mortmain was injurious to the Church.

Our horned prelates—in council are dumb—
And for fear of displeasure dare not say mumm.
They are so confounded with absence of the law
The Church and the Right Way are brought into awe.
—ANNALES.

When the Queen and Prince Edward went to France to arrange matters concerning the homage claimed for the Duchy of Guienne, she met Mortimer, who was raising an army to counteract the influence of the de le Spencers; and, landing at Orwell (in Essex) was joined by the followers of the late Earl of Lancaster. The King fled to the West seeking to reach Ireland but was driven back to the Welsh coast whence he fled to Kenilworth and Parliament declared him to be deposed. Bishop Orleton, of Hereford, preached before the Queen, the Prince, the Duke of Aquitaine and Mortimer touching the reason of the Queen's coming and the cause of the Army, taking as his theme "My head grieveth me" (II Kings iv. 9) "which authoritie he brought to such a question that a vaine and slouthful head ought necessarily bee taken away from the administration of the Kingdome, neither ought it to bee bound with any hurtful bonds to a hypocrite.—ANNALES.

This was in 1325. Two years later, Prince Edward issued writs for a fresh Parliament; but, as the barons had obtained the Great Seal, more regular writs were issued in the name of the King. When it met, Orleton preached on the "Theame" "Vox populi, vox Dei", and raised the question as to who should rule over them— the father or the son. Melton of York, Ross of Carlisle, Heath of Rochester, Gravesend of London and Reynolds, were in favour of the first, till Stratford of Winchester exhibited six articles against him and him of Canterbury veered round to the side of the son, who refused to accept the Crown till his father had abdicated, which he did at Kenilworth. (1327.)

The third Edward had his share of trouble with the Church; but his mother was successful in appointing Berilly as Bishop of Exeter although the Pope upbraided Reynolds for assisting at his consecration. On the death of the Archbishop, he was succeeded by S. Meopham (1327) who held a council that agreed upon accepting the doctrine of the Immaculate Conception and passed censure upon any one who should hinder the hearing of ecclesiastical cases in Church Courts. When the King sought to profit by the confiscation of the estates of rebels in Durham, the Bishop (Louis Beaumont) successfully resisted his claim on the ground that the Earl Palatine had the same rights as the King within his jurisdiction.

The King renewed the claim to the throne of France through his mother, but the Parliament of Paris decided upon Philippe V as the rightful heir. John XXII, seeing that war was imminent, as the French had seized many strong places in Normandy, sent two cardinals (one was Benedict Gaetano, afterwards Boniface VIII) to secure peace and arrange for the two kings to carry on a crusade; but, Edward sent Stratford to inform the French King that, though the cardinals still spoke of peace they meant war; he (Edward) would withdraw his claim on being guaranteed peaceful possession of his fiefs and the withdrawal of support to the Scots.

In 1333, King, Pope, and the monks of Canterbury were united in the choice of John Stratford (who was succeeded at Winchester by Orleton of Hereford in spite of Edward's dislike of those who had assisted at his father's deposition) who held a Synod at London at which he advocated the sentence of greater excommunication against all rebels as traitors; blamed churchmen for their extravagance, prohibited the farming of Church lands and benefices by laymen; obliged monasteries to provide for the poor and unappropriated parishes, restrained the costs in archidiaconal procurations and denounced the hindrance in the matter of collecting tythes and clandestine marriage between minors.

Convocation voted a tenth towards the French war and, following the example of his grandfather, Edward, to prevent treachery and the export of coin to France caused "to be confiscated all the goods of the Priories Aliens in England, that is to say such Priories as were celles to any monastery in France. He let out the Priories to Farme, with all their lands and tenements and rented them at his pleasure; for the space of three and 20 years; in the which time diuers of these Priories were purchased of the King, made free, and newly founded (as it were) by Englishmen, as Titbury in the Castle, and other: the residue not changed, were in the fiue and thirtieth year of king Edward's reyn againe restored to their lands—as shall be shewed when I come to it. . . .

"And on the sixt of Februarie following (1361) the king restored to the Priories Aliens their houses, lands and tenements as by his patent may apear, as followeth. Edward by the Grace of God king of England, lord of Ireland and Aquitaine, to all these presents, &c. Although the Priories of Montacute. in the county of Somerset (by reason of the warre between vs and France) with all the lands, tenements, fees advowsons, together with the goodes and chattels belonging to the same, hath ben of lately taken into our hands, and by vs farmed and rented forth as appeareth by diuers patents.

"Now, therefore since peace is betwixt us and the noble prince, our most deare brother, the king of France, wee for the honour of God and Holy Church, restore to the said Prior, the Priorie with all the lands, tenements, fees, advowsons and whatsoeuer else belonging to the same, to hold the same as in free manner as they held it before. And withall, forguie and release all arrearages of rents which might be due vnto us by reason of any former grants. In witness &tc the first of Februarie the 35 yeere of our reign".

"Similar grants were made to the priories of North-ampton, Arundel, Cameringham, Otriton, Pritewell, to the number of one hundred and ten in England, besides others in Ireland, Normandie and other parts of France."—ANNALES.

Stafford, of Canterbury, had been instructed to collect the moneys advanced by the merchants of Brabant and to pay the King's debts; but, as his collectors were slow in doing their duty, Edward sent a notary to him to warn him to take care of the bonds and either discharge them or cross the seas and remain abroad till the money was paid. He elected to go abroad, and he wrote to the clergy to the effect as that he had attended too much to temporal duties and he would henceforth follow the example of St. Thomas. He informed the King of what he had done and urged him to appoint a committee to inquire into the alleged embezzlement of the moneys, offering to stand a trial "saving the honour of Holy Church and the dignity of his order." Edward then accused him of malversation and removed him (with Northburgh of Lichfield) from Office and arrested Willoughby (ex-Chief Justice of the Common Pleas), Sharshall (Justice of the same Court), several clerks in Chancery, Lord Wake and Richard de la Pole. The Archbishop took sanctuary in Canterbury, where he held a Synod, prohibiting the clergy to pay the ninth sheaf, and, again likening himself to St. Thomas, declined to appear in the Court and wrote to the King, whom he addressed as Rehoboam, demanding a trial of his peers and was accused of being the cause of the failure of the French expedition through his withholding the necessary funds in the Famosus

Libellus. When Parliament met in 1341, as he was about to enter the House of Peers, he was ordered by the Chamberlain to repair to the Court of Exchequer to hear the accusation against him. Demanding time to prepare his defence, he told the bishops that he intended to clear himself before a full House and the peers decided that no one of their number should be tried except by themselves. In a full Parliament, the clergy then demanded exemption from the jurisdiction of lay courts, the observance of the charters and the release of imprisoned clerks and the Commons the imposition of oaths upon ministers of the Crown to keep the laws and the release of all old debts to the Crown.

In 1349, the monks of Canterbury elected Bradwardine (a pious man and confessor to the King) but, his election was set aside in favour of John Ufford. As the latter died within a year of his election, Bradwardine was again elected; but in the same year Simon Islip (Secretary to the Privy Seal) became Archbishop of Canterbury and, after issuing a constitution to check clerical extravagances and maintain the liberties of the Church, was strong enough to make the Black Prince vacate a stall in St. David's cathedral which he had seized during a vacancy, and to condemn the Duchess of Kent for entering into a second marriage in spite of a vow of celibacy. He also complained to Parliament that when clerks were tried by judges they were too often deprived of the privilege of clergy. He founded at Oxford, Canterbury College for six regular and six secular clergy now merged into Christ Church.

England was visited by the dreadful scourge known as the "Black Death". Of the actual mortality caused by this plague we have no authentic details. Stow mentions it as being about one-tenth of the population which may have been 3,500,000 souls and says that in Spital Croft "more than fiftie thousand persons were buried but as that would place the population of London at about 100,000, this is incredible. In Yarmouth it is said that "57,104 persons, (excluding Mendicants and Dominicans) were buried in one year and the value of the benefice fell from about £116 to £40."—ANNALES.

The principal authentic sources of information concerning the mortality are the manorial rolls and the lists of inductions and in the county of York one-half of the priests died and in the diocese of Norwich two-thirds of the benefices changed hands.

Piers Plowman thus described the state of the Church:

> " Parsons and parisshe preestes
> Pleyne hem to the bisshopes
> That hire parisshes were povere[1]
> With the pestilence tyme."
>
> —*Vision*—165.

In order to fill up the vacancies in the parishes, the bishops had to ordain men of little or no education as we read of in the verses of William Langland

> " I be preese and parson
> Passynge thritty winter
> Any yet ken ich neither solne[1] or synge
> No seintes lives rede
> But I ken fynden in a feld
> Or in a furlong, a hare,
> Better than in Beatus Vir
> Or in Beatus Omnes,
> Construe oon clause wel
> And ken it to my parisshens,
> I kan hold love daies,
> And here a reves reckynynge;
> Ac in canons or decretals
> I kan noght rede a lyne."
>
> —*Vision.*—3317-3233.

[1] Poor

And schoolboys of the Middle (like those of later) Ages did not always avail themselves of their opportunities:

> " I have no kynde[1] knowynge quod I '
> Ye mote ken[2] me bettre,
> By what craft in my cors
> It comseth and where."
> "Thou doted daffe ", quod she,
> "Dulle are thi wittes,
> To litel Latyn thou learnedst
> Leod[3] in thy youthe."
> —*Vision.*—735-742

In 1362 the King forbade the collecting of Peter's Pence, which was the King's alms of one penny payable at Lammas by households that possessed thirty pence of their own of one "Maner of Cattel" and amounted in all to 300 silver marks.

He then ordered the prelates to appear before to arrange for the defence of the realm among themselves, the vicars, dependents and vassals in case of invasion.

Langham who had succeeded Islip (1366) was deprived of his temporalities for accepting a cardinal's hat and, after living in retirement at Oxford, accepted the see of Preneste and was succeeded by the inoffensive prelate William Whittlesey (1368).

The Church was powerful, as it included most of the nation who had brains and the prelates, and supported by Rome, did not shrink from bearding the King. It is true that the transference of the papal court to Avignon robbed the Roman Church of some of its lustre. There was also a national feeling against a foreign church that filled the best benefices with her creatures and made England a happy hunting ground for impecunious cardinals who held such rich plums in the Church as the

---

[1] Natural.   [2] Teach.   [3] Ignorant man.

Deaneries of Lichfield, Salisbury and York and the Archdeaconry of Canterbury, reputed to be the richest piece of preferment in Christendom. Besides this, the Popes appointed men three or four deep to English benefices by provision, taking from each the firstfruits, whether they lived to enjoy the benefice or not, and their collectors in London trafficked in dispensations, indulgences and pardons to such an extent that they sent some 20,000 marks (say £13,333⅓) annually to Rome.

"The brokers of the sinful city of Rome promote for money unworthy and unlearned catyffs to benefices of the value of 1,000 marks, while the poor and learned hardly obtain one of twenty. They present aliens who neither see or care to see their parishioners, despise God's services, convey away the treasure of the realm and are worse than Jews or Saracens. The Pope's revenue from England is greater than that of any other prince in Christendom, God gave His sheep to be pastured and not to be shaven or shorn."

After the victory over the French at Crecy in 1346, the strong feeling against aliens was increased and three years later when Clement VI demanded that two of his cardinals should be provided for by the gift of English benefices, Edward wrote to him to protest against such a usurpation of the royal prerogative. This resulted in the passing of the Act of Provisors (1351) which declared that the king and all other lords are to present unto benefices of their own or their ancestors' foundations "and not the Pope of Rome". This was followed in 1553 by the first Act of Praemunire—the first serious attempt of revolt against papal pretensions by which any one suing in the Court of Rome for a benefice or carrying an appeal from an English Court of Law to the Curia was liable to forfeiture or outlawry.

When the King ordered a census of the foreigners holding English benefices to be taken, the number was incredible and nearly all were non-residents. When he sent a deputation to Avignon to complain of this and to beg the Pope to desist from appointing by means of reservations and provisions, stating that many of them were cardinals and enemies to the country, Urban made a decree against "the heaping together of many benefices or spiritual promotions by one man for the execution of which he sent commandment to the Archbishop of Canterbury" (Islip) "and by him all his suffragans, to certify in writing the names, number and quality of every clerke, benefices or livinges in their several dioceses, and it was found that at that time, the cleargie of England exceeded all the Nations in bearing of offices about the king and common weale in the place of Justice and other, as appeareth by one which the B. of London then made, of many beneficed men at that time abiding within his diocese. Some had XX benefices with cure, and some more, and some of them had XX prebends besides other great dignities. As Wil. Wicha, who in the yeere of the deathe of Wil. Edington B. of Winchest. was made general administrator of Spiritual and temporall things pertaining to ye Bishoprick, and the next yeere was made B. of Winchest. this Wicham, besides ye archdeaconry of Lincoln, & provestship of Welles, & the parsonage of Manihent in Deuonshire, had twelve prebends; Simon Langham, archbishop of Canterbury and chancellor of England; John Burnell, Bishop of Bathe and treasurer of England; William Wicham Archdeacon of Lincolne keeper of the priuie seale; David Weller parson of Somersham, Master of the Rolles, serving the king Edward in the Chancery fortie yeres and more. Ten beneficed priestes Civilians and masters in chancery; William Mulse Dean of St. Martins le grand, chief Chamberlain of the Exchequer, receiuer of the king's treasure and jewels; William Askby, archdeacon of Northampton, chancellor of the Exchequer;

William Dighton, prebendary of St. Martin's, Clearke of the privie seale; Richard Chesterfield, prebendary of St. Steuens and treasurer of the kings house; Henry Snatch, parson of Aven or Oundal, master of the kings robes; Ihon Newenham, parson of Fennistanton, chamberlain of the Exchequer and keeper of the kings treasury and iewels; Iohn Rounceby parson of Hardwicke surveier and controller of the kings works; Thomas Brittingham, parson of Ashby, treasurer of the king for the parts of Guisnes and the Marches of Caleis. Iohn Troye treasurer in Ireland, diuers ways beneficed in Ireland. All these are certified in the diocese of London at that time."—ANNALES.

A few words concerning William of Wykeham; the great pluralist of his age.

Born about 1323, he was educated at Winchester under the protection of Sir Ralph Sutton and was known as "the Second Euclid" from his great knowledge of geometry. After being made undernotary at Winchester Castle at the age of twenty, he was transferred to the King's court and made keeper of Rochford in Hampshire during the minority of William Botreux, one of the justices in eyre for Wiltshire and Hampshire, steward of the King's works at Henley and East Hampton and surveyor at Windsor (1356) with power to impress men not engaged in the royal works at the Tower, Westminster and Dartford. His first benefice was that of Pulham which he received in 1357 and was worth £35 (say £420 of the present value of money) from the King who had escheated it from the Bishop of Norwich (then under suspicion of having committed manslaughter and robbery); but, as he could not obtain possession of it till some four years had elapsed, he was granted a pension of £20. He afterwards received a stall in Lichfield, and was made surveyor of Hadleigh and Leeds Castles, Eton, Littlejohns, Guildford, Shene, Eltham and Langley. In 1361 he became prebendary of Hereford, Broomyard,

G

Aberwgwylli, Llanwybrewi, St. Andrew's (Auckland), Beverley, and Oxgate in St. Paul's (which he exchanged for that of Tattenhal), St. David's, the Royal Free Churches of St. Mary in the Castle (Hastings) and St. Stephen's; he exchanged the Archdeaconry of Northampton for that of Lincoln and was made Canon of York, Bridgnorth, St. Patrick's (Dublin), provost of the fourteen prebends of Combe in Wells, and parson of Meheniot in Cornwall.

In order to remedy the ignorance of the clergy who had been appointed after the ravages of the Black Death, he maintained at his own cost seventy scholars who were distributed among the colleges at Oxford. Froissart mentions him as a "priest called Sir William de Wicam —by him everything was done and without him nothing was done". From this we can understand the quotation from a tract entitled, "Why poor priests have no benefices" (at one time attributed to Wycliffe but written after his death). "Lords will not present a clerk able of cunning of God's Law and good life and holy example . . . but a kitchen clerk or a fancy clerk or wise in building castles or worldly doing though he cannot well read his psalter".

CHAPTER SIX

THE LIFE AND TIMES OF JOHN WYCLIFFE

Several John Wycliffe's—Taxation of the Clergy—Wycliffe sent to Bruges
—The Duke of Lancaster—Wycliffe Becomes an Anticurialist—Simon
of Sudbury—The Good Parliament—Tracts—Disgrace of Wykeham—
Colleges at Winchester and Oxford—Wycliffe's Articles—Five Papal Bulls
—Trial at St. Paul's—Death of Edward III—Richard of Bordeaux—
Trial at Lambeth—Peasant Revolt—Translation of the Bible—Opposi-
tion to it—Langland and Sir Thomas More—Transubstantiation and
Celibacy—Courtney at Oxford—Council of Blackfriars—Final Summons
of Wycliffe—His Illness and Death—Trial of Haxey—Banishment of
Arundel—Quarrel between Bolingbroke and Norfolk.

WE know but little of the family and early days of John
Wycliffe, and that little is obscured by the fact that there
were several of that name flourishing about the same
time. Among these we may mention:—

1. John Wycliffe, of the diocese of York, who petitioned
the Curia to appoint him to a prebend and dignity in
that Minster, and received the stall of Aust in Westbury
Collegiate Church.

2. John Wycliffe, a fellow of Merton.

3. John Wycliffe, provided with a stall in Lincoln,
which he lost through neglecting to pay the first-fruits.

4. John Wycliffe; rector of Mayfield; a benefice that
Islip wished to annex to Canterbury Hall.

Our John Wycliffe is said by Stow (in his manuscript
of Leland) to have been born at Hipswell (Ipreswell) in
Richmondshire; but the MS. at this point is imperfect,
and Hearne says it is Spreswell, identified by Lodert, as a

vanished hamlet near Wycliffe-on-Tees. If this is correct, he may have been a member of a family immortalised by Sir Walter Scott, one of whom

> " glossed the cause
>   Of Commons Covenant and Law
>   And Church reformed:"
>   —*Rokeby.*—XI.

As, in 1384, he wrote that he was then sixty years of age, he appears to have been born in 1324, and was educated at Balliol College, then most frequented by students from the North. He is said to have been Warden of Canterbury Hall, and to have been expelled from that office by the Benedictine Langham, who replaced the secular clergy of that house by regulars. This is uncertain, but, he is said to have made an allusion to it in his "de Ecclesia" (cap. XVI. p. 370), and it was assumed by the monk of St. Albans (Chron. Aug., Rolls Series 115), and by his opponent William Woodford (Fasc. Łin. p. 317), and Stow says:—

"He (the Duke of Lancaster) called unto him a certain divine who many yeere before in all his acts in the Schools had inveighed against the Churches for that he had been deprived by ye Archbishop of Canterbury from a certain benefice that he unjustly (it is said) was incumbent upon within the citie of Oxford. His name was John Wycliffe, who with his disciples were of the common people called Lollards, they went barefooted and basely clothed, to wit, in course russet garments down to the heeles, they preached especially against monks, and the religious men that had possessions etc.; among other things he desired ye bishop of Rome to have authority to excommunicate any person, and that any priest might absolve such one as well as the Pope."—ANNALES.

He attracted many hearers to listen to his lectures on Philosophy, and, becoming Master of his College, resigned that position to take the rectory of Fillingham (1361), and has presented to the Canonry of Aust in the Church of Westbury on Trim.

These changes enabled him to continue his lectureship at Oxford (to which there was no stipend attached) and he frequently preached to large audiences at St. Paul's Cross.

The temporal lords were angry at the large number of pluralities held by the clergy, as they had suffered much during the French Wars while the latter remained at home, and demanded the dismissal of the clerical ministers of the Crown and William of Wykeham (of Winchester) and Brington (of Exeter) were replaced by the scarcely less clerical Sir Thomas Thorpe (Master of Pembroke Hall, Cambridge and the friend of Lancaster) and Sir Richard le Scrope as chancellor and treasurer on the understanding that for the future the chancellor, treasurer and lord privy seal should be laymen.

In 1371, Parliament again insisted upon the observance of the Charters, and levied a tax of £50,000 upon all priests, even the poor charity priests. To raise this, it was calculated that a tax of 23s. upon each parish would bring in the required sum till the great council sitting at Winchester found that instead of their being 40,000 parishes there were only 9,000 and the assessment was raised to 116s. "the greater helping the less"; owing to extreme poverty, the parishes in Suffolk and Devonshire were only assessed at 112s. 7d. and 112s. 10¼d.

It would be interesting to give some details of the number of parishes thus assessed in the various counties.

County	No. of churches	Amount		
Norfolk	808	3,674	16	0
Yorkshire	540	3,171	12	0
Suffolk	515	2,926	0	0

County	No. of churches	Amount
Essex	400	2,259 18 0
Somerset	391	2,267 16 0
Devonshire	343	2,149 0 0
Sussex	284	1,647 4 0
Cambridgeshire	171	997 12 0
London	110	637 0 0
Chester	97	(Being a county palatine, was not taxed)
Middlesex	63	365 8 0
Rutland	44	355 4 0
Westmorland	32	185 12 0

The gross amount thus received was £51,000.

In 1372, Wycliffe was joined to the Duke of Lancaster to go with the Bishop of Bangor, to meet the papal envoy on matters connected with Provisors. His importance is shewn by the fact that his name came next to that of the Bishop and that he was allowed 20s. a day for his expenses. But little came of this as, although the Duke promised to endeavour to obtain the repeal of that act and the discontinuance of presentations by writs of "quaere impedit" if the Pope would agree to protect sealed benefices from provision, allow bishops to compel alien clergy to repair their churches, and excuse English litigants from appearing at Rome during the continuance of the war, the King, Court and Parliament were alike interested in the then existing state of affairs as they could retain their share of Church patronage by negotiating with the curia rather than with the bishops and chapters.

This official employment changed the course of his career and, his eyes being opened to the tortuous policy of Rome, he did not hesitate to declare Urban "the proud and worldly bishop of Rome" and the "most accursed of clippers" and "purse kervers". On his return he was

presented to the living of Luttersworth, and resigned
that of Ludgershall as he said it was not lawful to hold
more than one cure of souls but, retained the canonry.

On the death of Whittlesey (1373), Simon (Thibbald)
of Sudbury, Gilbert and Courtney were translated from
London, Bangor and Hereford to Canterbury, Hereford
and London.

The Black Prince, worn out with the duties during the
French War and the Governorship of Guienne, returned
to England and, with the aid of Wycliffe and the Friars
obtained the return of the Good Parliament of 1376
which was presided over by Sir Peter de la Mare, a
relation of the Abbot of St. Albans, and prayed for the
auditing of the public accounts, the prosecution of the
war with France, the preservation of peace at home, the
free election of members (in many cases simply nominated
by the sheriffs and mayors), the annual election of sheriffs
and the removal of evil councillors (among whom were
Lord Latimer, Richard Lyons the King's lapidary (who
were accused of malversation and fraud, especially the
maladministration of the war with France and the buying
up of the King's debts) and Lady Hastings (Alice Pierce
—the daughter of a Hertfordshire gentleman who was
continually in litigation with the Abbot of St. Albans) from
the King's Council. Again we will borrow from Stow:—

"The Commons demanded the dismissal from the court
a certain woman called Alice Pierce, by whom much
familiarity she had with the king, was the cause of much
mischief in the realme, she exceeding the manner of
wommin, sate by the doctors in consistories; perswading
and diswading in defence of matters and requesting
things contrarie to lawe and honestie to the great dis-
honour of the king."—ANNALES.

About this time Wycliffe issued two tracts, the best
known of which is the "Determinatro quodam magistii
Johannes Wycliffe contra unum monachum" in which he

attacked the right of the clergy to hold property since neither Christ nor His Apostles had any possessions, and stated that as all the property belonged by right to the Saints so the sole authority to hold possessions arose from righteousness from which the Pope had fallen short and sinned and had forfeited his right to the tribute from England. In the "Dominium Divinum" he declared that from that time he would abandon philosophy and devote himself to the study of Divinity and Theology and set forth that God in His nature is Essential and Eternal and that all human lordship is derived from Him and granted by Him to His vicars on terms of perfect obedience; making a broad distinction between "dominion" and "power", as the latter might be exercised by wicked man by His permission as Suzerain of the Universe, that as the Popes had sinned they had lost all claim to the tribute from England and that as God was supreme over spiritual matters, so the king was supreme in temporal matters and had power to withhold the temporalities from a delinquent clergy.

This teaching pleased Lancaster as the leader of the anti-clerical party and, as he was unpopular through his ill success in France, the Bishops of London and Lincoln and Lords Arundel, March and Salisbury, with Sir Guy Brian and Henry le Scrope, met the Commons to devise some plan of bringing about a better state of things; but, they were defeated by the intrigues of Alice Perrers.

The Commons then accused the Bishop of Winchester (Wykeham) of misappropriating money passing through his hands while he had held the Great Seal (1361-1371), of having reduced the fine levied upon Sir John Grey for having alienated certain property without the King's consent; of having taken bribes from the Free Companies; of having released certain French prisoners (especially the Duke of Bourbon to whose influence he was said to have owed him the See of Winchester); of having failed to relieve Ponthieu and of having bought up the King's debts. When he admitted having altered the record of the fine levied upon Grey as he thought it was excessive, but denied having gained any personal advantage from it, Justice Skipworth produced an Act of Parliament which declared that any alteration or erasure to the prejudice of the King in the rolls of the courts, was punishable by a fine of one hundred marks for every penny omitted.

He was fined 960,000 marks (£192,000) and sentenced to banishment within twenty miles of the King's Court and his temporalities given to Richard of Bordeaux. Courtney of London (as dean of the Southern Province) urged the clergy in Convocation to refuse to pass any Act until this sentence was remitted and Wykeham was restored to his position. "Seeing the lawes of the land to bee handled, not according to lawe, but as it pleased certain persons, and being destitute of all man's help, he turned to womankin, providing not only for himself, but also for the oppression and losses of his church. Therefor, knowing yt Alice could do all things that shee would and ther was not any man that would in any way resist her will, he requested for her help; he offered her money. he promised her great friendship if she would help his bishopricke forth of such trouble. she promised to despatch his cause and not refusing what was offered, went to try if any mark of loue remained in the King. He therefore that long ago had bin taken with her love, enticed by her speeches, supposing nothing to be denied her now that she was asked; against ye duke's will. he commanded his temporalities to be giuen to him againe; and so the bishop, by right or wrong, recovered all that was lost. But he had to provide three gallies with fifty men at arms each and fifty archers, or the wages of 300 men for three months."—ANNALES.

This compelled him to dismiss his household and discontinue the maintenance of his seventy scholars; but between 1377 and 1380, he purchased lands in mortmain (including the manor of Stoke Perrers the property of Lord Hastings, husband of Alice Perrers) to endow his prospective colleges at Winchester and Oxford.

In 1378 he gave a charter for the erection of " Seynt Mary College of Wynchestre by Winchester" for a warden and seventy "pore and needy scholars to study and be proficient in Grammaticals or the art and science of grammar", as a means of educating men to take the place of the incumbents who died during the Black Death and subsequent visitations of sickness, which was not opened till 1394. Judging from his first nominations the words "pore and needy" implied not those who were destitute, but rather to the sons of yeomen, citizens of London and Winchester and the middle class generally, being in straitened circumstances. The more famous foundation was that of the "Seynt Marie College of Wynchestre in Oxford" likewise for a warden and the seventy scholars whom he had previously distributed in other colleges to study theology, canon and civil law and the arts. This foundation now consists of a warden, and thirty-six fellows.

Wycliffe continued in his denunciations of the Roman Pontiff declaring that the Roman Church was no more the head of the Churches than any other Church was; that Christ gave no more authority to St. Peter than to the other Disciples and Apostles; that no bishop should excommunicate any man for injuries done to him, but only in the cause of God, and that no man would be the worse for such a sentence unless he had excommunicated himself by his own act; that temporal lords and governors might take away the temporalities from a delinquent Church and that in many cases it might be a meritorious act to do so; that the Gospel was a sufficient rule of life and that no rule imposed by holy and godly men could add to its perfection; that neither Pope or Bishop should have any prison for offenders against Church discipline, but that all such should be left at personal liberty.

This aroused the wrath of Gregory XI who issued five bulls against him and his teaching. That sent to the University of Oxford expressed grief and surprise that the Chancellor and scholars, being the recipients of so many graces and privileges granted by the Holy See with such a knowledge of the Scriptures which should have made them ardent defenders and champions of the Orthodox Catholic Faith, should have allowed tares (lolium) to spring up among their "clean corn and neglect to destroy their seeds". He specially mentioned John Wycliffe, "professor of theology" (would we were not compelled to add also a teacher of errors) "who burst forth into such detestable madness as to put forth certain erroneous and false propositions and conclusions savouring of heretical pravity and plainly tending to subvert not only the constitution of the Church, but also of all systems of civil government", which opinion he not only dared to avow, but to preach publicly or "rather to vomit them out of the poisonous dungeon of his breast, defiling some of Christ's faithful ones with the slaver of his rabid mood, and leading them astray from the right path of faith headlong to perdition". And, this, too, in the Realm of England "glorious in her power and resources and still glorious for her faithful affection for the True Faith and full of men noted for their knowledge of the Scriptures, gravity of manner, eminence in devotion and in the defence of the Catholic Faith". He then proceeded to order the University to arrest him and those who followed his teaching and keep them in custody till it might be convenient to send them to Rome. It also gave particulars of the points upon which he was to be questioned, and directed that his answers should be sealed and forwarded to the Pope. Lest he should attempt to take refuge in any exempted house, the law that all heretics should be examined by the bishop in whose diocese they might be living was abrogated. The University refused to arrest an Englishman at the bidding of a foreign sovereign and persuaded him to take up his residence in Blacknell Hall. Other bulls were directed to the two primates, telling them to warn the "old king", Joan of Kent (widow of the Black Prince) and the lords of England of the danger and disgrace that would befall the country if they were negligent in this matter.

Courtney of London persuaded the Lancastrian Simon of Sudbury to summon Wycliffe to appear before him in St. Paul's on February 19th, 1378 and the Reformer was brought into the church attended by friars (who looked upon him as their champion against the secular and monastic clergy), and the common sergeant. Owing to the crowd, the Duke of Lancaster and Lord Percy had great difficulty in forcing their way through the press of people and Courtney told him that had he known he would have behaved in that fashion he would have prevented him from entering the church. When the Duke requested that Wycliffe might have a seat as he had much to answer, the Bishop replied that it was most unusual for one to sit when being interrogated by his ordinary, and evoked the retort that "he would pull down the pride of him and of all the bishops of England and that his trust of his parents would avail him nothing", to which the prelate answered that he did not place his trust in his parents nor in any living man but in God in Whom he ought to trust, and the angry Duke declared that he would rather pull him out of the church by his beard than suffer such things at his hand. The Londoners, of whom but few knew anything of the teaching of Wycliffe and thought that their Bishop must be right, became so turbulent that the court had to be broken up without any result being arrived at. They then went next to destroy the palace of the Savoy which would have been sacked but for the action of the Bishop.

Soon after this, Edward died deserted by all save an unknown priest and Alice Perrers. It is narrated how the latter spoke cheerfully to him, promising him a quick recovery and the coming pleasure of hawking and hunting; but, when she saw the end was fast approaching, she is said to have stripped him of the rings that he wore for his "majesty" and left him. The priest remained and approaching him heard him say the word "Jesus" just as he drew his last breath. There is considerable doubt as to the meaning of this narrative, as the only other person present was the priest who probably was inimical to her and the rings might have been a death-bed gift.

Edward was a benefactor to the Church and founded a nunnery at Hertford, the Maison Dieu at Calais, a hall for poor students called King's Hall (since merged into Trinity College at Cambridge), a college for a dean, twelve secular canons and fifty prebendaries and twenty-four poor knights at Windsor and refounded the college of St. Stephen's at Westminster, which he endowed with £50 a year for a dean, twelve secular canons and twelve vicars.

He was succeeded by his eleven year old grandson—Richard of Bordeaux, in 1377. Richard is one of the most disappointing characters in English history. The son of a brave father and a brilliant, if versatile, mother, he spent the early part of his boyhood in the gay court of Guienne, where he acquired a love of painting, music and poetry and was well versed in the lays of the Trouvères of the Langue-d'Oc. He did not lack courage; but he was weak, easily influenced by those who flattered him, violent in his uncontrolled temper and lavish in his expenditure. He chafed under the control of his uncles of Lancaster and Gloucester and ruled first constitutionally but was obstinate and tyrannical during the later part of his reign.

To carry on the government, the Commons appointed a council, including the Earl of Arundel and Michael de

la Pole (afterwards Duke of Suffolk), but rigorously
excluded his uncles of Lancaster, Gloucester and York.
The care of his person was entrusted to his mother, Joan
of Kent, who was favourable to the teaching of Wycliffe.
His first Parliament petitioned for a remodelling of the
Council of State by the addition of eight members and
the appointment of his personal attendants " to secure him
receiving a proper education."

Wycliffe was again summoned before the bishops—this
time in Lambeth Palace Chapel where, deserted by his
former allies the mendicant orders, he defended his
teaching in writing and with more caution than he had
shown in St. Paul's, questioned the right of the clergy to
hold benefices in free and perpetual alms; attacked the
pretensions of the papacy; stated that any priest could
administer or withhold the Sacraments; confirm and
ordain and that excommunication was harmless except
to an enemy of God. On the receipt of a message from
the Princess of Wales, the judges appeared as "men like
shaking reeds and their speeches were as soft as silk and
oil and were struck with such dread that they were as
men who heard not and were without proof in their
mouths". So was the court that met to try the reformer
again broken up and he escaped without one word of
reproof.

It is difficult to give any one reason for the popular
outbreak known as the "Peasant Revolt" of 1381. After
the ravages of the Black Death, labour was so scarce that
much of the land got out of cultivation, to remedy which
Parliament passed the First Statute of Labourers by
which any one, not having lands upon which to subsist
and not being artisans was compelled to work for the
first person who shall claim their work, and employers
giving more than the wages current in their district
before the Pestilence were liable to fines amounting to
three times the money paid in excess. Not only was the

country filled with landless labourers; but the lords, impoverished by the expenses of attending the King during the French war were fain to grant freedom from a servile tenure for money rents of the land. The country, too, was infested by returned soldiers who were unwilling to work and sought a livelihood by handing over the country and seeking subsistence by threats and violence. In order to secure the necessary labour the lords gave their stewards orders to look into the deeds of enfranchisement in order to find flaws in them. This discontent was increased by the Band of Poor Teachers organised by Wycliffe, and was modelled on the ideas of SS. Dominic and Francis, travelling in the country, mixing with the people, professing poverty without indulging in mendicancy and preaching the Gospel in the churches of which the incumbent was favourable to, and elsewhere in the market places, in gravel pits, and wherever they could gather an audience. Many thus, doubtless, preached the pure gospel, but others may have spoken upon the philosophic view of the great teacher and refrained from drawing attention to the religious side. Langland describes how the "Sely man" complained that he could find no man who "fulle beleeveth" and that the Friars were equally faithless and appearing to be "in vestibus ovium" but within they were "wilde wer-wolves that did not invite the people to live" and had gone far from the rules of SS. Dominic and Francis, thinking only of obtaining pecuniary privileges from Rome and neglecting the poor man with his toes coming out of his shoes and his fingers from his mittens who followed the plough drawn by four miserably thin oxen urged onward by his wife who walked beside him, cutting her feet in the frozen clods, clad only in a sheet, while her children, lying in a cradle in the furrow, cried in a "kareful note". And again, Piers had no "puny pullets to buy but two green cheeses, curds and cream and an oaten cake with two loaves of beans and bran for his children," while "labourers who had no land would not dine on yesterday's greens, perry ale or bacon."

This distress was followed by the imposition of a poll tax varying from 10 marks payable by the duke of Lancaster to 4*d*. by every priest, monk and persons of humble origin, with an assessment of 2*s*. for every beast owned by married couples. This was rigorously exacted, but failed to produce more than £20,000.

England was seething with discontent, and was ready to fall a prey to any agitator who might see his way to make capital from such a state of affairs. One of the best known of these was Sir John Ball, who was supposed to have been a disciple of Wycliffe, but would rather seem to have been influenced by Rolle or Fitz Osbert, as one of his favourite sayings was taken from the former:

"When Adam delved and Eve span,
Who then was the gentleman?"

He had been imprisoned several times before 1381 for travelling about the country spreading sedition, and who was afterwards known as a preacher in a political, rather than a religious, fashion, especially to addressing the people as they were leaving church after Mass. Several letters have been attributed to him, in one of which we can find traces of the teaching of Piers Plowman.

"John Shepe, sometime Mary Priest of York and now of Colchester, greeteth with John Nameless and John Miller and John Caster and biddeth them that they beware of Gillesborough alias Gitenborough and stand well together in God's Name and biddeth Piers Plowman to *go to his work* and chastise Nob the Miller and take with him Io Truman and all his fellows and no more. Io the Miller hath ground small, small and the King's Son of Heaven shall pay for all. Beware ye ye woe, know friend from foe, have ynough and say Hoe! And *do ye well and do better*, and flee sinne and seek peace and hold therin and so saith Io Truman and all his fellows."—ANNALES.

It appears to have broken out simultaneously in Kent, Essex and East Anglia, whence the insurgents marched to London, executing all lords, lawyers, justiciars, quest-mongers and those who had the slightest suspicion of having a knowledge of Latin, French or Flemish, insisting upon the acknowledgment of King Richard and the abjuration of a king named John (Lancaster) and the legality of any tax save the time honoured fifteenth.

The men of Kent, reaching Canterbury, immediately released John Ball from the archiepiscopal prison and elected him to be their archbishop as there was none more worthy of that honour as he declared that all bishops canons, rectors and curates should be slain; that no tythes should be paid to any rector unless the payer was richer than the payée and should always be withheld unless the latter were of a better life than the former; that all ecclesiastical property should be confiscated except some £116,000 (the sum at which Wycliffe had placed the income of the Friars) to be devoted to the maintenance of seven hundred friars without distinction grant in order that there might be some provision for the administration of the Sacraments.

He added all men were free from birth, and that bondage was the result of sin, of man's oppression and contrary to the Will of God.

While the men of Kent encamped on Tower Hill, the men of Essex and Hertfordshire bivouacked in Smithfield.

The latter plundered the goldsmiths' shops in Lombard Street and the Duke of Lancaster's palace in the Strand and, forcibly entering the Tower, brutally murdered the Venerable Archbishop Simon of Sudbury, Sir John Hayles (Master of the St. John's Hospital), whom as Treasurer, they looked upon as the author of the Poll Tax.

H

Richard, then aged fifteen, rode among them, accompanied by Sir William Walworth, promising that no land should be let at more than 4d. an acre and when it had been less should be reduced to the lower sum, that all servile tenure should be abolished, and all who had taken part in the rising should receive pardon; but the lords refused to ratify these terms, as they said the King could not grant what was not his to give; hundreds were hanged and the remainder remained in the same state as before.

Many have blamed Wycliffe for not using his influence in preventing this, but the probability is that he knew little or nothing about it, as he was engaged with Hereford and Purvey in translating the Bible from the Vulgate into English.

. As early as 1378, he had written in his "Pastoral Office", "The worthy Reaume of France, notwithstanding al letting hath translated the Bible out of Latin into Freynsshe. Why sholde not the Englisshe do so? As the lords of Englande have the Bible in Freynsshe, so it were not ageyn reasoun that they hadden the same sentensis in Englisch."

It is not known what part he took in this work, but the Old and the greater part of the New Testaments are attributed to him; and Nicholas de Hereford is accredited with part of the Apocrypha as far as Baruch iii—20 after which are these words "Hic explicit Nicolai de Hereford" said to have been written just before he was summoned to appear before the Consistory. The whole work is said to have been revised by Purvey and finished between 1388 and 1400 and some one hundred and seventy Manuscripts still in existence date from the end of the fourteenth century.

There was great opposition to this work. Langland wrote:

Thanne hadde wit a wife,
Tha hotte[1] was dame Studie.
That was lene of lere[2]
And of liche[3] bothe;
She was wonderly wrothe
That witte had this taught;
And all staring dame Studie
Any wisdome to telle
To flatteres and to foles,
That frenetic be of wittes ?"
And blamed him and banned him,
And bad hym be stille,
With swiche wise wordes
To wissen[4] any sotte,
And seide, "Noli mittere man,
Margerie perles.
Among hogges that han
Hawes at wille;
Draffe[5] were hem lever
Than all the precious peree[6]
That in paradise waxen[7] "

—*Vision.*—5526–5619.

Foxe relates how the Archbishop Arundel commended Anne of Bohemia (consort of Richard) for having in her possession many translations of the Scriptures which she had read in Latin, German and Bohemian and Wycliffe wrote in his *Threefold Bond of Love* that would be "luce-ferian folly" to accuse her of heresy for having done so".

More than a century after the death of the Reformer, the enlightened Thomas More wrote the following: Ye shall understand that ye great archheretic John Wycliffe, whereas the Holy Bible was long before his dayes by vertuous and well learned men translated into ye English

[1] Named.	[3] body.	[5] refuse.	[7] grow.
[2] face.	[4] teach.	[6] stones.	

tong and by good and godly people with devotion soberly, well and devoutly read, took upon him of malicious purpose to translate it anewe. In which translation, he purposely corrupte ye Holy Text, maliciously planting therin such wordes as might in ye reders serve to the proofs of such heresies as he was about to sowe. . . . I have myself seen an can show you Bibles fair and elde, written in Englische, which have been known and seen by ye bish of the dioces and left in leman's hands and woman's." But we are uncertain as to what More intended to allude, for besides certain separate translations (mostly commentaries before and after the time of Rolle) we have no previous attempt at a complete translation of Holy Writ.

He then attacked the Doctrine of Transubstantiation as being blasphemous as it led men to idolatry, and illogical as it premises the existence of an accident before that of the substance. Stow thus writes:

"John Wickliffe, parson of Lutterworth in Leicester, laboured in his teaching to prove that after consecration in the Mass by the Priest, the Bread and Wine were then present as before. Christ being present as an assistant. as in every place but more expecially; and that the same Bread and Wine be not more worthy than any other bread excepting only for the blessing of the Priest and therefore he affirmed that Churchmen were deceived in honouring the same bread—which was a thing without life, for anything that has life was better than that which lacketh life."—ANNALES.

He also attacked the doctrine of celibacy and urged that the clergy should be amenable to lay tribunals as trials in Church Courts were conducive to conspiracy; that tythes should be withheld from delinquent clergy; that monasteries should be converted into asylums for the poor; that no preferment should be given to alien clergy who were likely to convey the treasure of the realm across the seas; that no clerk should hold any secular office; and that imprisonment for excommunication should be abolished; and, complaining of the increasing power of the papacy, upheld the enforcement of Praemunire and Provisors, and even petitioned the King to be allowed to hold a public discussion on matters relating to the Eucharist and the withholding of tythes from delinquent clergy.

The easy going Lancastrian, Sudbury, had been succeeded by the bold and energetic Courtney (1382) who as Legatus natus, claimed to represent the Pope as the Chief of the Oxford University and, anxious to suppress the teaching of Wycliffe, ordered the Vice-Chancellor to summon a court at which Berton, Rygge and five doctors (three being monks) forbade the "new" teaching of the Eucharist to be taught or practised under pain of the greater excommunication. From this the rector of Lutterworth appealed not to the King but to the Pope; but his lay supporters, willing to join him in his anticlerical teaching and recommending the doctrine of Evangelical Poverty as regards the clergy, were unwilling to involve themselves in the condemnation meted out to heretics in respect to Transubstantiation; and Lancaster himself was obliged to renounce the Wycliffite heresy at the altar.

Rygge was unable to carry out this decision, and, when the University appointed Nicholas de Hereford and Ryppington to preach in St. Frideswyde's on the feasts of the Ascension and Corpus Christi, the townsmen armed themselves to protect the officers of the University against the Friars.

So strong was this feeling that the commissary of the archbishop wrote to say that he dared not carry out his orders for fear of his life. Ryppington spoke strongly against the monks, and said that Holy Orders were in a better condition when they were but nine years old than they were a thousand years later, and William Jones (in the class rooms) said that the Wycliffites were holy priests under the protection of John of Gaunt and that the only idolatry was at the altar.

To strengthen his hands, Courtney held a council at Blackfriars. Scarcely had the clergy (among whom were himself and the Bishop of Durham and Nantua, six doctors and eight bachelors of Divinity and seventeen doctors and two bachelors of Civil Law) assembled, than the whole building was shaken by an earthquake. Some would have adjourned the meeting, but the Archbishop said it was a good sign as it showed that the earth was trying to purge itself of foul vapours so the Church would purge herself of heresy; but not without much trouble. Out of twenty-four of Wycliffe's articles ten were pronounced heretical and the remainder erroneous; the doctrine of Transubstantiation was confirmed and the Scriptural authority of the Mass; the supremacy of God over the devil; the authority of the Pope over the faithful independent of the word of the emperor; the recognition of the successors of Urban; the legality of priests to hold secular offices; the necessity of auricular confession and the right of bishops to pardon were maintained. When Wycliffe heard of this (1382) he said that as "Herod and Pilate had agreed to make a heretic of Christ, so it was easy for the regular and secular clergy to make one of a simple Christian." Ashton, Hereford and Ryppington were condemned in contumacy; and Rygge was obliged to kneel before the proud prelate and deny that Jones had spoken as a wise man should have done; but, when ordered to publish the findings of the Blackfriars' council in Oxford, said he did not dare to do so for fear of his life, and was told that the University was a "fautour" of heresy, since it would not allow the Catholic Truth to be published within its boundaries.

Wycliffe was not present at the Council but wrote to Parliament to induce it to withdraw from obedience to the bishops except in purely ecclesiastical matters, to prevent aliens holding English benefices and to confiscate Church lands rather than impose fresh taxes.

In 1383 he was again summoned to appear before Courtney, and is said to have recanted, but evidence seems to point out that he presented a fuller exposition of his doctrine in English. In that December, he was stricken with a palsy while elevating the Cup at Mass. A monkish chronicler writes:—"John Wickliffe the origin of the devil, the enemy of the Church, the idol of heretics, the image of hypocrites, of the storehouse of lies, being struck by the terrible judgment of God, was seized with a palsy throughout his whole body, and the mouth, which was to have said large things against God and the Holy Ghost, was miserably drawn aside and offered a miserable spectacle to behold: his tongue was speechless and his head shook, plainly showing that the curse that God had ordered against Cain was also inflicted upon him." For twelve months he lay on a bed of sickness: but when visited by four friars and the same number of aldermen, he raised his head and declared that he would recover and live to expose their errors as they were, he said, with their followers, *ipso facto* excommunicate.

The Papacy was in an unsatisfactory state. On the death of Gregory XI in 1376, the cardinals elected the bishop of Bari who took the style of Urban VI, and the French princes of the Church withdrew to San Angelo, declaring their lives were in danger. The next day, they returned to the Vatican and acknowledged Urban, who offended them by urging them to live in a less ostentatious manner, rebuild the churches of their title and avoid simony. They again withdrew and elected Robert, Count of Geneva, who is known as the anti-Pope Clement VII. Then was Christendom divided: England, the greater part of Germany and Italy remained true to Urban, while France, Spain, the Netherlands, Scotland and Navarre sided with Clement. Urban was angry with

Richard for not raising an army to enable him to hold his own against Clement and, thinking that Wycliffe was the cause, cited him to appear before the Curia. This he was willing to do and petitioned the King to allow him to go to Rome as soon as he could leave his bed. In the meantime, he wrote to the Pope to say it had long been his desire to have the opportunity to explain his news to him in order that, if they were correct, they might be confirmed, or, if erroneous, corrected. He added that as the chief vicar of Christ upon earth he was of all men the most bound to follow His teaching and as He and His Apostles were the poorest of mankind, casting aside all civil authority, he hoped that he would surrender his temporal power and induce his clergy to do the same, as "Truth is not arrived at by the mere counting of heads but the most exact imitation of Christ."

He died the last day of December, 1384, and was buried at Lutterworth.

Again to quote Stow:—

"This year Master John Wickliffe, sometime student in Canterbury College in the University of Oxford, person in Lutterworth in Leicestershire, having been greatly vexed with a palsy for the space of two years, died the last of December and was buried at Lutterworth" where his remains were undisturbed till after the Council of Constance (in 1414) when Bishop Fleming of Lincoln had them exhumed, burned and cast into the river Swift a tributary of the Avon.

> The Avon to the Severn ran,
> The Severn to the sea;
> So Wycliffe's dust was borne abroad
> As far as waters be,
> —FULKER FULLER.

Richard insisted upon one Haxey, a prebendary of Southwell, being tried for treason in presenting a petition complaining of the maintenance of my bishops and Clerks in the royal court. Being condemned, he was claimed by Arundel as a *persona Ecclesiæ* and imprisoned till the coronation of Henry IV. And the Archbishop himself was condemned to banishment for treason, being replaced by Roger Walden, the King's treasurer, by provision.

The King's cousin, Henry of Bolingbroke, Duke of Hereford, and the Duke of Norfolk accused each other of treason and then both were condemned to banishment, the one for seven years and the other for life.

In spite of clerical opposition Lollardry was increasing, being supported by the Queen, Lords Salisbury and Montague and such country gentlemen as Latimer, Clifford and Sturry and the merchants of London who hoped to see a change in the bad financial policy of the crown till Knyghton (a canon of Leicester where the influence of John of Gaunt was great), said that if one met three persons, two were sure to be Lollards who boldly preached that the Seven Sacraments were but unprofitable symbols, that the intention and not the Ceremony constituted marriage, that the churches were synagogues of Satan, that the practice of Transubstantiation was a feigned miracle and led to idolatry, that baptism was to be avoided lest an impure priest should corrupt the child, that celibacy among religious men and women was unnecessary and led to much scandal, that auricular confession led to priestly arrogance, that prayers said over Water, Bread, Wine, Wax, Stone walls, Altars, Images, Crosiers, Staves, and Vestments savoured of witchcraft and should not be tolerated; that Masses were unscriptural, that the trades of goldsmiths, sword cutlers and armourers were unlawful as they led to bloodshed and luxury and that the use of gold and silver chalices was unnecessary. But above all they claimed that the church governed by popes, cardinals, canons, rectors, vicars, monks and friars who enriched themselves at the cost of a starving peasantry was not the Church founded by Christ and His Apostles who were examples of Evangelical Poverty and that St. Peter would not have taken money from those who confessed their Faith.

So bold had they become that they actually pasted placards upon the doors of the principal churches, including those of St. Paul's and Westminster Abbey.

> Plagunt Anglorum genus crimeni sodomorum
> Paulus fert horum sunt idola causa malorum
> Surgunt ingrati, corrupto semine nati
> Mentum prelati, hoc defensare parati
> Qui reges estis, populis quicunque præestis
> Qualiter his gestis gladys prohibere potestis.
>
> —ANNALES.

On this, Courtney and Brayebrook (of London) hurried across the sea and beseeched the King to return to help the Faith and the Church, "So incredibly afflicted by the Lollardes (as they termed them) howe they might take away all the possessions of the Church; and what was worse, how they might take and destroy all Canonical sanctions."—ANNALES.

After appointing the Earl of March as heir presumptive and hurried back to England where he summoned the Lollard chiefs, Sir Thomas Latimer, Sir James Mountague, and Sir Richard Sturry before him, sternly rebuked them, threatening them if they henceforth favoured the Lollards, or in any wise afforded them comfort, he would extremely punish them; he took an oath of Sturry that from henceforth he should not hold such opinions, which thing being done, the king said: And I sweare to thee that if thou ever violate thine oath, thou shalt die a shameful death; others hearing such roaring of the Lion plucked in their heads and lay close.

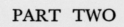

PART TWO

LOLLARDRY AND COUNCIL OF CONSTANCE

In the following pages we intend to pursue the History of the Reformation in the Church of England from the Death of Wycliffe to that of Henry VIII a period of some century and a half.

The time of Richard II had seen the voice of the people —inarticulate as it may have been—asserting itself and the growing knowledge of the Scriptures spreading among them. These were to bear fruit in the time occupied by the present volume to the extent that the papal power was abolished in England and the Church became a national one; quite independent of Rome and at the same time the Kings of England shook off their glorious isolation and became the arbitrators of Europe. But this did not happen without serious trouble, and the neglect of matters purely English for the glories of the foreign field led to the misrule of the sixth Henry, the attempt to make the monarchy an absolute personal one by Henry Tudor and the assumption of spiritual and temporal power by "Bluff King Hal" and his claim to govern the state in obedience to the Machiavellian policy of "l'état, c'est moi".

The Reformation as left by the last was temporal rather than religious and there was but little doctrinal difference between the Churches in the early days of that King and it was only in his last days that much alteration was made in the ritual.

And ther shal come a king
And confesse yow religiouses

And bete yow as the Bible telleth
For brekynge of youre rule;
And amende monyales,[1]
Monkes and chanons,
And putten hem to penaunce
Ad pristinum statum ire;
And barons with erles beten hem
Thorough Beati Vires teachyng
That hire barnes claymen
And blame yow foule
Hi in curribus et hi in equis ipsi obligati sunt.

And thanne freres in hir[2] fraytour
Shul fynden a keye
Of Constantyn's coffre,
In which is the catel
That Gregorie's god-children
Han evele dispended,
And thanne shal the abbot of Abyngdone
And all his issue for evere
Have a knock of a King
And incurable the wounde.
                    —*Pier's Ploughman—Vision.*—
                                6239.

We mourn not for our abbey lands, e'en pass them as
     they may,
But we mourn because the spoilers' hands found far
     richer spoils than they.
They cast aside as a thing defiled the remembrance of
     the just,
And the relics of our martyrs they scattered to the dust;
Yet two at least in their holy shrines escaped Spoilers'
     hands
And St. Cuthbert and St. Edward might well redeem a land.
                    —*Ecclesiologus.*—J. M. NEALE.

---

[1] Inhabitants of cloisters.   [2] their.

CHAPTER SEVEN

LOLLARDRY AND THE COUNCIL OF CONSTANCE

Return of Hereford—Deposition of Richard II—Coronation—Lollard Speaker—Degradation of Peers and Restoration of others—Death of Richard II—Religious Schism—Lollard Lords: de Hereford, Swinderby, Ryppingham—Thorpe's Testament—Martyrdom of Sawtry—Ill Estimation of Lollards—Canterbury Pilgrims—Institutions of Arundel—Burning of Heretics—Northumberland's Rebellion—Scrope of York—Message of the Pope—Henry and the Lollards—Chicheley, Pluralist—" quare impedit "—Loses Preferment—Projected Spoliation of the Church—Arundel's Warning—Death of Henry—Boniface IX—Clement VII and Benedict XIII—Innocent—Rival Popes—Council of Pisa—Henry V—Hallam—Alexander V—Oldcastle cited as a Lollard by Bishops—The Ecclesiastical Court—Escape from the Tower—Yorkist Plots—Capture and Death of Oldcastle—Danger to the State—Translation of Richard's Remains—Monastery at Sheen—Henry's " Chapel in France "—Advice to the Benedictines—Clemency towards the Families of Heretics—His Death—Marriage of Henry VI—Alexander V—John XXIII—Councils at Rome and Constance—Election of Martin V.

WHEN Richard of Bordeaux banished Henry of Bolingbroke he treated him with great liberality, giving him a sufficient income to support his position as a prince of the blood and guaranteeing him succession to the Lancastrian estates; but on the death of his uncle he confiscated his lands on the plea of paying for the Irish war. Although forbidden to hold any communication with the exiled Arundel, Hereford frequently met him and it is said the former paid more than one visit to England to see how political events were shaping themselves. The two obtained permission from the King of France to visit the Duke of Brittany and, being joined by certain malcontents, including Sir John Oldcastle—one of the lords appellants who had sought to put a limit upon the tyrannical conduct of Richard—embarked with fourteen other knights to recover his lost position and estates. Landing at Ravenspur, the Duke disembarked and was welcomed by the Earl of Northumberland; and, being joined by some 60,000 men, he no longer concealed the fact that he sought the crown. Richard and Henry went to London, one on the stately war horse and the other on a sorry nag, and the first went to pay his devotions at the tomb of his father and mother in St. Paul's and the second was sent to the Tower.

Before leaving for Ireland Richard had summoned a Parliament that duly met. Facing the chair of estate was a double series of chairs, those on the right for the lords and those on the left for the commons. The formal act of abdication being read, Bishop Marks of Carlisle alone had the courage to protest against its legality as having been signed under duress; for this he was shortly afterwards deprived of his See. The names of the various members of the royal family were then read out. Those of the Duke of York and his son (the Duke of Aumerle) were negatived and that of the Earl of March (whose father had been acknowledged by Richard as heir presumptive and had been slain in Ireland) was passed over in silence; perhaps because he was a minor; but that of Bolingbroke was received with acclamation.

Lord Percy then drew the ring from off the finger of Richard and placed it on that of Henry who, ascending the chair of estate, listened to a sermon from Arundel on the text "Vir dominabatur in populo". The unfortunate King whose presence was no longer required was led away to Leeds Castle and thence to Pontefract.

Arundel was then restored to the archiespiscopate and allowed to proceed against his successor Walden as an intrusionist; but afterwards he consecrated him to the See of London.

As the title of Henry was not without flaw (the real heir after Richard being the Earl of March through Philippa, daughter of the Duke of Clarence, second son of Edward III), he determined to have a sumptuous coronation, and the Archbishop used for the first time the sacred oil said to have been given by the Blessed Virgin to the exiled Thomas à Becket by whom it was concealed (after his return) in an empty tomb. Having been lost sight of, it was discovered by a hermit and placed among the treasures of the Tower. The Archbishop refused to have it used to cover up Richard's breach of faith with his subjects by a second coronation.

The Commons of his first Parliament elected Sir John Cheyney (who had been ordained a deacon but had abandoned the stole for the sword and had served in the French wars) as Speaker; but, as he was suspected of Lollardry, he was replaced by Sir John Durward. The proceedings of the last Parliament of Richard were declared null and void. The Dukes of Aumerle, Surrey and Exeter were reduced to the rank of Earls while Lords Arundel, Suffolk and Warwick were restored in blood, and Bowet (afterwards Bishop of York), Clifford of London (Lord Privy Seal) and Mitford of Salisbury were declared loyal subjects and Arundel was allowed to proceed against Walden as an intruder; but in 1405 the former consecrated his former foe to London.

Scarcely had he been crowned than the Earl of March revealed a plot to assassinate him at the jousts to be held in his honour and Lords Salisbury, Gloucester, Huntingdon and Lumley, with many others were executed. Richard died shortly afterwards either from violence or voluntary starvation or from the intense cold of his prison at the age of forty-four. His body was conveyed with great pomp from Pontefract, the face being bare and the procession halting in every considerable town through which it passed from evening till after Mass on the following

I

day. In London it remained for two hours in the Cheap where it was seen (says Froissart) by 20,000 citizens. When it was taken on to St. Paul's for the Requiem Mass, Henry acting as pall bearer, it was buried in the College founded by Richard himself at King's Langley. In spite of this, many declared that the late King had fled to the Hebrides whence the regent of Scotland invited him to take up his residence in Stirling Castle, and this rumour was believed in for twenty years.

England was divided into two groups; those who wished things to remain as they were and those who would reject tradition and look to the Scriptures as the only guide to Faith.

The followers of Wycliffe were generally known as Lollards, a word either derived from "lolium" (corncockle) or from the word "lollen," to sing softly. In the beginning of the XIV century there was in the Netherlands a sect—a branch of the Franciscans—known as Fratricelli, Spirituals or Beghards, whose duty led them to tend the sick and bury the dead, to renounce all papal authority and to profess (at least for others) evangelical poverty, urging the clergy to renounce their tythes and temporalities as they said the Church that exacted payments from the starving peasantry for spiritual offices was not the Church founded by Christ.

In England the followers of Wycliffe rapidly increased, till he said that two-thirds of the parish priests were in favour of his doctrines, and Knyghton (Canon of Leicester, where the influence of John of Gaunt had been predominant) said that, out of every three men one met, two would be Lollards; but probably these were of the patriotic party which were in favour of the refusal to pay the tribute demanded by Urban and thought but little of the question of Transubstantiation.

After the Peasant Revolt of 1381 the Duke of Lancaster retired more or less from public life and his place was taken by him of Gloucester as protector of the popular rights and in a tract attributed to Wycliffe, but evidently written after his death (perhaps by the chaplain to the Duke), the writer urged his patron to rub away the rust of error from the opinions of either party.

Among the more important Lollards were Lords Salisbury and Latimer, Sir John Mountague who had removed images from his private chapel and left no instructions for Masses to be sung for the benefit of his soul, Sir William Clifford, Sir Thomas Latimer, who wished his body to be interred in a remote corner of the churchyard, with only two paters and providing no meat or drink but for those who were in want of them and Sir William Neville. Among the clergy, the principal adherents were John Purvey who had assisted Wycliffe in the translation of the Bible and after his death had preached in Bristol till he was inhibited by the Bishop of Worcester. He then engaged himself in translating his master's *Commentary on the Apocalypse*, and, recanting, was appointed to the vicarage of Hythe, which he resigned in 1403.

Nicholas de Hereford, likewise was an amanuensis of the Great Reformer and, being cited before the consistorial court, appealed to Rome where Urban declared his opinions worthy of death. The Roman curia objected to his being burned alive as he had gone there under a safe conduct and he was imprisoned till the mob drove the Pope from Rome and liberated him. He returned to England and was confined to the prison at Saltwood till he recanted before Arundel; again he was cited before the ecclesiastical court for advising an aged man to seek forgiveness for his sins from God alone and not to trouble about absolution from an earthly priest. He afterwards conformed and was made Canon of Hereford in which capacity he assisted at the condemnation of the Welsh protestant—Walter Brut.

Byhold on Walter Brut
That bisiloche they pursueden
For he seid them in the soothe
First to burnne the body
In a bale fier
and sythen thi sely[1] soule to slaine
And send hire to helle
      —*Piers Plowman's Creed.*—1309.

Falling under clerical displeasure he obtained letters of protection from Lancaster and died a Carthusian at Canterbury.

William Swinderby preached in the streets, in the market-places, in gravel pits, on commons, in fact wherever he could gather an audience upon the weaknesses and vices of the clergy and laity alike. Lancaster allowed him to live in a disused hermitage in his park, and when the bishop summoned him to appear before him he refused to obey unless he received a safe conduct to go and return, which was granted, much to the chagrin of the monks who had prepared a "bale" fire for his execution.

He denied the meaning attributed to his words, and promised never to preach again in the diocese of Lincoln unless it were to retract opinions of which he had been accused of uttering. He then retired to a deserted chauntry near Derwolsden, on the Welsh Marches, where he preached and administered the Sacrament in Both Kinds. He held forth on the faults of the clergy whom he said had a commission from God in addition to the episcopal license to preach the Gospel and that while baptism as administered by a godly man was good, it was harmful if so done by a wicked man, and declared that tythes might be withheld from delinquent priests.

[1] Pious.

Another noted man was Ryppington, who had defied Arundel at Oxford and, recanting at St. Paul's, became Bishop of Lincoln and was created Cardinal by the Council of Pisa; but, owing to the irregularity of the proceeding, never ventured to act as such.

The extreme school of Lollards was represented by William Thorpe, who was more than once summoned to appear before Arundel, and wrote bitter things against the clergy suggesting that bishops should work for their living and when old should be supported by charity. In his "Testament" he recognised the authority of the Church when exercised by godly men endowed with Christian virtues and graces; maintained it was wrong to swear by the New Testament as it was a creature of God; that music was harmful as it tended to distract men's attention from God; that when David mentioned musical instruments he intended to typify the Christian virtues and that the clergy should renounce their tythes and practise evangelical poverty. To these opinions others added more extravagant opinions, such as the necessity of abstaining from frequenting churches as the synagogues of Satan; from matrimony as the intent was more important than the ceremony; from baptism lest a child should be corrupted by an impure priest, from the observance of Sunday in favour of the Jewish Sabbath, and from placing images in churches lest they should become the abode of evil spirits. Some went so far as to decry the Sacrament as being conducive to idolatry.

William Sawtry when vicar of St. Margaret's (King's Lynn) had been suspected of heresy but escaped by recanting. Being appointed to St. Osyth's (St. Size) in London, he was again brought before the Church Courts as a relapsed heretic for saying it were better for a man to worship Christ rather than the Cross upon which He died; that priests should preach as well as recite the offices at certain hours; that it were more profitable to spend money on alms than to go on pilgrimages and to worship a man than an angel as Christ took upon Himself the likeness of the former. Being found guilty he was degraded from the priesthood and, being handed over to the secular power, was burned alive in Smithfield.

That Lollards were not held in high repute may be gathered from the lines of Langland and Chaucer—

> Thus ich waked, God wot!
> Whenne ich woneded[1] on Cornhulle.
> Kytte and ich in a cote
> Clothede as a Lollare
> And a lytel ich let by
> Leeve me forsoothe
> Among loleres of London
> And lewede[2] heremytes.
>
> *Vision.*—WHITTAKER. PASSUS V.

And again:

> For them that han hele[3]
> And here eyen syghte
> And lymes to laborye with
> And lolleres lyf usen,
> Lig ven ayeres Goddes lawe
> And love of Holy Churche.
> And thai aren beggeres
> And put arn there other beggars,
> In hele as it seemeth
> Ac hem wanted hire witt,
> And men and women bothe
> The wiche aren, lunatik Lollers
> And leperes aboute,
> And mad as the moon sitt,
> More other lasse.
>
> *ibid.*—Variation of lines 4621–4,658.

[1] Dwelt.　　　[2] Ignorant.　　　[3] Health.

Whether or not Chaucer was a Lollard, or favourable or unfavourable to their opinions, we know not, but he certainly had a good knowledge of the Bibles, as may be seen from quotations curiously intermingled with classical lore and the mention of the physician skilled in diagnosing diseases and learned in the writings of the principal medical authorities of the age but

"His study was but litel on the Bible"

and he gives an illustration of how eager they were to promulgate their opinions in and out of season;

"Sir, Parish priest, for Goddes bones,
Tell us a tale as is thy forward lore.
Can mochel good, by Goddes dignity"
The person him answered "Benedicte
What willeth this man so sinfully to swear,"
The host answered "Oh! Jenkin, be ye there?
Now good man," quod our host, "and hearkeneth to me."
"I smell a Lollar in the wind," quod he.
"Abideth by Goddes Passion;
We shall have a predication."
The Lollar her wil preache somewhat."
"Nay, by my father's soul her shal he nat preche;
We leeve in the great Gode" quod he.
"He wolden sowen some difficultie
Or springen Cockle in our clean corn".
                    —*Canterbury Tales.*— 2,606.

The unyielding Arundel then published his constitutions which provided that all Wycliffite books should be searched for and destroyed; that no priest should preach except in accordance with the Church laws; and then only with the license of his Bishop; that all schoolmasters teaching opinions contrary to the traditions of the Church should be subject to the penalties of the

Greater Excommunication; that all places where conventicles had been established should be placed under an interdict till all preachers and listeners had made their submission; that no preacher should question any doctrine already sanctioned by Mother Church or uphold any doctrine opposed to such teaching under the pain of the Greater Excommunication till he should have undergone penance and published his recantation; that no books written upon Divinity by Wycliffe (or by others after his time) should be taught in the schools until such books should have been authorised by the Universities; that no one should translate the Bible without episcopal license, that all decretals and constitutions touching the worship of the Cross and images should be punctually obeyed; that no clerk should officiate outside his diocese without letters of demission; that every master, warden or principal of any college or hall should make monthly inquiries into the opinions of all students under his charge, reform them if they were erroneous or, if obstinate, expel them under pain of being declared excommunicate or being deprived, and that no one should presume to speak the weaknesses or vices of the clergy.

As these proved to be fruitless, Parliament passed the Statute of de Comburendo Heretics by which all persons preaching or infected with heresy or possessing heretical books were liable to imprisonment during the King's pleasure and in cases of lapse to be burned on a high place in the presence of the people. Many suffered under this statute, which was only repealed in the time of Charles by the exertions of Jeremy Taylor and Chillingworth. Coke defended it on the grounds that as it was necessary to remove lepers to preserve mankind from contagion so it was advisable to prevent heretics contaminating a nation. When the Pilgrim Fathers left England to find liberty of conscience in the New World, they took this idea with them and mercilessly persecuted those who differed from them in their Puritanic Doctrines. So much for liberty. "How many crimes are committed in thy name!"

Although Richard had left a well-filled treasury amounting to something like £55,000 Henry was often short of money, being compelled to satisfy the necessities of those who had helped him to secure the throne and alienated the Earl of Northumberland by refusing or being unable to pay him certain sums expended in putting the Scots Marches in a state of defence. The Earl was assisted by Owen Glendower (the titular Prince of Wales), and drew into his toils the weak-minded Earl of March with whom it is said (perhaps without foundation) he signed a tripart treaty by which the second was to have the whole of the north of England, including Norfolk, while Glendower was to be Lord of ancient Cambria and Lord March of the rest.

He was joined by Scrope (Archbishop of York) who, when captured and asked why he was in arms against the King, replied that it was because he had been prevented from seeing Henry and that his purpose was good and commodious to his majesty if he only knew it. On his capture, the upright Judge Gascoigne refused to pass sentence of treason against a prelate and said that it could not be done by any court in England; but Justice Fulthorpe was more complaisant and the prelate was executed with all the horrors of death for that crime in mediaeval England. When Pope Innocent heard of this, he ordered Arundel to pronounce excommunication upon those implicated, but, as it involved the King and nearly all the nobility, he did not dare to do so and the King sent the bloodstained coat of mail with which the Bishop was clad at the time of his capture to the Pope with the words: "Lo, we have found this; know whether it be your son's coat or not".

Previous to his exile Henry had lost his wife—Mary de Bohun—and, while in Brittany, had become infatuated with the duchess who on the death of her husband obtained from the anti-Pope—Benedict XIII—a dispensation to marry an unknown person within the fourth degree of kinship—meaning Henry. The London *Chronicle* says that she obtained his love through "sorcerie and negromancy". The casuists of both schisms disapproved of this marriage—those adhering to Boniface because he had been uncertain in his religious views, having been brought up in the court of John of Gaunt who favoured the Lollards; and those of Benedict as they considered Henry a schismatic; but the latter quieted her conscience by assuring her that she might associate and even communicate with the followers of his rival provided she remained true to him in heart.

Among the great churchmen of the period was Henry Chicheley, born at Higham Ferrers about 1364. (In 1445 he petitioned Eugenius IV to be relieved of the cares of the arch-see as he was nearly eighty years of age.) He was educated at New College and proved to be one of the greatest pluralists in the history of the English Church, rivalling Beket and Wolsey in this respect. Before he had been ordained by the Bishop of Derry (as Suffragan to him of London) he held the benefice of Llanvarchal and had practised in the Court of Arches and in that of Chivalry in the absence of the Lord High Constable. He received many preferments, being rector of St. Stephen's (Wallbrook), maintaining his appointment to the Archdeaconry of Dorset against Bubworth (Master of the Rolls) and holding the benefices of Sherston and Brington, besides being prebendary of Salisbury, Nantgwilli, Lichfield, St. Martin's le Grand, Lincoln, Abergwili and the nun' chapels at Shaftesbury and Wilton and was approved chancellor of Salisbury to hold which, having been appointed by Provisors, he had to obtain consent from

Parliament. In 1408, he obtained the See of St. David's by the same means, being allowed to retain all his other preferments.

Mitford died soon after he had presented him to the stall in Salisbury, and the presentation was left incomplete. Henry had promoted Hallam (Haloman) from York to Salisbury and issued a writ "quare impedit" as the installation had not taken place during the occupancy of the See by the grantor. The case was argued before the whole bench and when he produced the bull appointing him to St. David's, Judge Horton said that he had been permitted to hold his stall for which he had performed homage to the King after the enthronement of Hallam and that he was protected by the bull. Thurming said that the Pope could not alter the law of England and when his brother Hankford argued that "papa omnis potest" he granted that it might have been so formerly but that he could not alter the law of England at his will. "Jeo ne ferre disputation del poiar de l'appost mes jeo ne scay coment par ses bull' il poit changer le ley d'engleterre". Culpepper said that the Statute of Praemunire and Provisors were passed to protect the King and other patrons in their rights and to restrain papal encroachments. Another Justice—Till—remarked that since the law provided for a voidance in patronage during the interval between the death of one bishop and the enthronement of another, he could not see how the "Apostle" could oust a patron from his rights (as to do so would be to alter the whole law of inheritance in England) any more than the King could give a man permission to hold property after taking monastic vows. To this Hankford replied that the "Apostle" might give a man a dispensation to hold more than one bishopric with the consent of the patrons; but when Skene remarked that if that happened the King might withhold the temporalities, he was answered by Hankford that the

"Apostle" might in certain cases change the course of the law and prevent the occurrence that would naturally follow. "What say ye, suppose the 'Apostle' (before a man becomes a professed monk) granted him a dispensation to hold his benefices." Said Hill, "In that case I should be deprived of my patronage." In spite of these varied opinions the case was decided in favour of the crown and Chicheley, deprived of his several benefices, received, by royal permission a bull enabling him to transfer his chancellorship and his stall in Lichfield to his nephew—a minor and a lay student—and, after being enthroned in St. David's, served the King as ambassador to France.

It may be noticed that in these proceedings the Pope is never referred to as such or as sovereign pontiff wielding the delegated powers of the Chief of the Apostles or Successor of St. Peter, but as the "Apost", "Noster saint Pier", and "St. Peter".

Henry was compelled to reward his followers to such an extent that he was often short of money and the Commons were averse to raising funds by an increase of the then existing taxes, looking rather for help from the ecclesiastical resources. In 1410, he ordered his sheriffs to prevent the return of lawyers to the "Unlearned Parliament" from which he demanded a sum of £146,000, of which £130,000 was to be devoted to strengthening the defence of the realm to be expended under the supervision of the Duke of York, the Earls of Somerset and Westmoreland and six other lords (including the Lords Privy Seal and Treasurer), four knights (including the Wycliffites Cheyne and Savage) and four representatives of the city of London.

The Commons affirmed that as they supplied money for the government of the kingdom and went in person to the King's wars at great cost besides putting themselves in "daunger and jeopardie", while the clerks sat idly at home, the extra money should be furnished from the lands of the bishops and richer abbots and that the King should be content with confiscating such estates which they divided into three classes estimated at £20,000 each.

I. The possessions of Christ Church and St. Augustine's at Canterbury, Shrewsbury and St. Osyth's.

II. Those in the North except Fountains and Rivaulx and of

III. The religious houses at Dover, Battle, Coventry, Daventry (Daintry) and Thorney in the Isle.

Out of these funds were to be provided 15,000 priests without distinction of rank or privileges, 15 earls, 15,000 knights and 6,000 esquires who were to receive 3,000 marks a year and four ploughlands. 100 marks and the same quantity of land and 40 marks and two ploughlands respectively, while with the residue there were to be founded 100 hospitals, leaving the king an income of £20,000 a year.

In addition to this we have the foreshadowing of the Poor Law Relief as each township was to provide for those of its poor who could not earn their living.

As might be expected, Arundel strongly opposed this measure, saying that while the laity contented themselves with granting fifteenths, the clergy granted tenths and, as large landowners, sent more men into the field from their temporalities than did the greater and smaller lay proprietors; beside praying night and day for the prosperity of the King and the success of his army. When Cheney said that he put but little store upon the prayers of the Church, Arundel replied that he "could see which way the wind lay and could plainly see to what end the realm would come when the suffrages of the Church whereby the Godhead was wont to be appeased were thus set at nought—surely a kingdom devoid of prayer and devotion could never stand firm". He added characteristically that those who should attempt to take away the possessions of the See of Canterbury should not be without punishment if his life were spared and, kneeling before the King, he reminded him how gracious God had been in helping him to the Crown and how he had promised to maintain the Church and her ministers in their respective rights, urged him to think twice before he broke his oath to his personal danger and begged him to continue to preserve her in all her happiness and liberties she had enjoyed during the reigns of his predecessors and to continue to govern in the name and fear of that King to Whom all earthly kings owed their power. Then from his seat he addressed the Commons and told them that, although they had recommended the King to confiscate Church property, they should remember how their predecessors had granted Edward III the possessions of the alien priories, promising him that thereby he might obtain great riches "worth thousands of pounds in gold"; yet he was never the richer by half a mark as his advisers had appropriated all that wealth for their own benefit, and now he thought that they desired the present plundering to satisfy their own covetousness rather than benefit the King since if (God forbid they should) they fulfilled their wicked design, he would not be one farthing the richer the next year following and "surely I would rather let my head be cut off, rather than the Church should be destitute of the least right that pertaineth to her". The reply of the Commons is not recorded; but, Arundel won the favour of certain lay lords who prevented this being carried out into law.

Henry was victorious in the French wars, but during the last years of his age was afflicted by a mysterious disease and returning to England in 1413, paid a visit to the shrine of St. Edward before which he was discovered in a state of unconsciousness. Being taken to the Abbot's lodging he asked where he was and, being told that he was in the Jerusalem Chamber, said that he had taken the vow of the Cross intending to rescue the Holy Places from the infidel after he had settled affairs in France and it had been foretold that he should die in Jerusalem.

The Papacy was not without its troubles.

On the death of Urban VI (1380), the Roman cardinals elected Boniface IX who became master of the city of Rome and curtailed the privileges of the citizens by nominating the magistrates and, to carry on his war with the Visconti's of Milan, rigorously exacted the payment of the annates which (in England) only affected the bishops and richer abbots and those clergy appointed by Provisors.

Eleven years later Clement VII died and the Avignon Cardinal elected Peter de Luna (an Aragonese nobleman) who had been created cardinal by Gregory on account of his uprightness and, after having voted for Urban, had transferred his allegiance to Clement), known as Benedict XIII.

On the death of Boniface, the Cardinals at Rome took a collective oath to do the utmost in their power even to laying down their pontificate if elected, provided Benedict would do the same, to end the schism.

In 1404, Innocent VII was elected and made the mistake of recognising the astute and crafty Ladislaus instead of the loyal, if feeble, Louis of Anjou as king of Naples. The citizens of Rome, seeing that the schism was diminishing the number of pilgrims, sent a deputation (which was barbarously treated), to the Pope's nephew and the Orsini and Colonna indulged in private warfare.

Innocent created several cardinals among whom were Peter Philargis (a Cretan, afterwards Alexander V), Angelo Corrar (a Venetian, afterwards Gregory XIII) and Otto Colonna (afterwards Martin V).

Thus western Christendom was rent in twain, England, Germany and part of Italy recognising Innocent and

France, Castile, Aragon, Navarre, and the rest of Italy following Benedict.

The University of Paris took a moderate view and recommended the rivals to call a council to which they should surrender their dignities and should either one or the other be re-elected—or a third party—the unsuccessful candidate should retire into private life and recognise the successful one.

On the death of Innocent, the King of France sent an army to invest Avignon; but, Benedict escaped down the Rhône and took up his residence in Peniscola where the Dukes of Orleans, Burgundy and Berri urged him to lay down the tiara; but he replied that this would be an act displeasing to God as if he abdicated, he would be false to a trust to which he had been elected by the suffrages of many good men; but he would be pleased to discuss his position with any one who might be elected as his rival if a suitable place should be agreed upon.

This was difficult as, perhaps, both Popes were determined not to come to an agreement and Gregory fled before the army of Ladislaus of Naples (who proposed he should abdicate and retain his Venetian preferments) to Lucca, where as he created fresh cardinals, his associates fled and joined those of Benedict, who wrote of his rival as "Angelo Corrar whom some of this pernicious heresy call Gregory" and was in turn called by him "Peter de Luna whom some call Benedict during this miserable schism".

A new factor arose in the person of Baldessare Cossa —of whom we have many accounts, probably all equally false—who had studied at Bologna and went to Rome declaring he was seeking the Papacy.

With the aid of Philargis and the dissentient cardinals, he called a council at Pisa at which were present fourteen cardinals (out of twenty-six), the patriarchs of Alexandria, Antioch, and Jerusalem, twelve archbishops, fourteen bishops, eighty-seven abbots and priors and five hundred representatives of the Dominicans, Augustinians, the knights of the Temple, of St. John and of the Teutonic Orders, of the universities of Oxford, Cambridge, Paris, Montpellier, Bologna, Ferrara, Cracow and Cologne, and of princes of England, France, Spain, Portugal, Sicily, Cyprus, Brabant, Pomerania, Thuringia and Brandenburg.

Henry sent two knights—Rixon and Colville—with a letter to Gregory complaining of the continuance of the schism which he attributed to the sloth and avarice of the temporal princes to whom the material sword had been entrusted for the defence of the Church and who had failed to put an end to it by courteous persuasion, blaming him for breaking his word by creating fresh cardinals and begging him to put an end to the present state of affairs and preventing further slaughter of Christians, stating that in the bishopric of Liége alone 30,000 persons had lost their lives in the struggle between the rivals.

Hallam took with him some memoranda drawn up by William Ullathorne who, favourable to the teaching of Wycliffe, had continued in the Church, insisting upon the necessity of maintaining peace within it which would be obtained by the Popes preaching themselves and sending out preachers to make a Holy War upon the passions of mankind which (according to St. James) were the root of all divisions and wars. He spoke of the irregularity of Papal elections; of the prevalence of simony within the Church; of unnecessary appeals to Rome and the promiscuous granting of licenses and indulgences that increased licentiousness; of the employ-ment of clerics in secular matters and enjoining a more reverend manner of conducting Divine service. They then summoned Benedict to attend but refused to admit his proxies and, declaring him and Gregory to be deposed,

K

elected Philargis who had been the "rich bishop of Milan, the poor cardinal and was about to become the beggarly Pope" as Alexander V in 1409.

Gregory fled to Austria and, at Cividale di Friuli, declared both Benedict and Alexander schismatic and scandalous and took shelter with the Malatesti, at Rimini, where he created Gabriel Condalmar a cardinal (afterwards Eugenius IV); and the three pontiffs from their restricted territory acted as sovereign pontiffs and freely excommunicated each other.

The reign of Henry V of Monmouth (1413–22) was noted for the successful prosecution of the French Wars and the Persecution of the Lollards. When Henry of Bolingbroke returned to England he was accompanied by Sir John Oldcastle, who had been banished for attempting to limit the Royal prerogative. Having married the heiress of Lord Cobham, he was called to the upper house and made governor of Hay and Brecknock castles; and, after building and endowing a chauntry for three priests, embraced the doctrines of Wycliffe, boldly avowed these principles, declaring that before that he could never resist sin, and his estates and those of his wife were placed under an interdict as he filled the pulpits with Lollards. In 1413, he was accused of heresy and, being a personal friend of Henry, was sent to Windsor to be convinced of the errors of his opinions. The principal piece of evidence against him was the possession of two books, concerning which Henry said he had never seen such horrible writings against the Mass, and he defended himself by saying he had scarcely read two pages of them, assuring the King of his loyalty as always being ready to serve him as he knew he was a Christian king bearing the sword of justice for the protection of the virtuous and the punishment of evil-doers, that, next to God, he owed him his whole obedience and was willing to submit to him in the future as in the past all that he had "of nature and fortunes" and to fulfil his commands in the Name of the Lord: but concerning the Pope, he owed him neither suit or service as he knew him to be the great Anti-Christ, the Son of Perdition, the open Adversary of God and the Abomination of Desolation, sitting in the High Place. In the end, he offered to clear himself of all charges against the King by the compurgation of one hundred knights and esquires or by single combat. Finding he was already condemned, he fled by night to his castle of Cowling which he had provisioned as for a siege. Notices were placed on the castle gates and on the doors of the cathedral and other churches in the diocese of Rochester and the interdict on his estates was renewed. Appearing at Leeds Castle, he was examined by Arundel, Beaufort of Winchester and Clifford of London to whom he acknowledged the obligation of confession and penance followed by the Communion; but refused to worship images as they were merely the means of bringing home to the people the sufferings of Christ and His saints denied the efficacy of pilgrimages as all were pilgrims to weal or to woe and said that journeys to Canterbury and Jerusalem were useless unless the word of God were observed. This did not satisfy his judges who ordered him to sign a declaration on his belief in Transubstantiation and obligatory confession to a priest; the acknowledgment of Gregory as the true successor of St. Peter and the vicar of Christ; the meritorious value of pilgrimages and the worship of saints and images. The trial was adjourned to Blackfriars where he refused to seek absolution from Arundel as he had never injured in word or deed or thought, and, holding out his arms, craved pardon from God whom he had grieved in his youth by pride, covetousness and lechery, and added that he had been punished obeying the Laws of God and not for breaking those of the Pope. He again refused to believe in Transubstantiation in that the Bread and Wine being changed by the act of consecration which he declared had been introduced into the Church since her corruption by the Donation of Constantine, said that he would honour the Cross of Christ by carefully preserving it and ended by a long oration declaring the Pope and all his bishops to be the head and tail of Anti-Christ. Being handed over to the civil power, he was sent to the Tower for forty days (to give him time to recant) whence he managed to escape.

In 1414, the Earl of March revealed a conspiracy to murder the king at the Christmas masque to be held at the palace at Eltham. He hurriedly left for London and ordered the mayor to call out the watch and shut the gates to prevent the movement of all suspected persons. Riding in the garb of a Crusader, he put himself at the head of the citizens and at St. Giles' Fields met some 25,000 men gathered together to plunder St. Paul's, Westminster Abbey and all the Friaries. Twenty were slain and sixty, among whom were Sir Roger Acton, Beverley the preacher and Sir John Brown, were captured. Cobham escaped and avoided capture although a reward of 500 marks was placed upon his head. The next day, a party of Lollards was defeated at Harringay under the command of one William Murles, a maltster or brewer of Dunstable, clad in rich armour with gold spurs as he had been promised the title of duke and the lands of St. Albans abbey by Cobham who is supposed to have fled to the Marches of Wales where he was engaged in hatching conspiracies to overthrow the house of Lancaster.

Henry's position was precarious, not only had he to face the Lollards but he was menaced by the partisans of the family of York, and when he was at Southampton (1415) fitting out an expedition against France, the Earl of Cambridge, and Lords Scrope and Northumberland conspired for his death, after which the young Lord March was to be taken to the borders of Wales and crowned with a diadem brought to England on the marriage of John of Gaunt to Constance of Castile and mortgaged to the Duke of York. The conspirators were arrested and executed.

When Cobham heard of the sailing of the King of France, he came out of hiding and was defeated near Worcester by Lord Burgoyne. His chaplain revealed his headquarters as being in an old house, within the double walls of which were hidden arms and a banner with Cross, the Scourge and the Nails of the Crucifixion. When Parliament heard of his defeat, they refused to separate till he was captured and he was taken, severely wounded to London in a "whirlicote".

The Duke of Bedford presided over his trial for heading an insurrection at St. Giles' in the Fields and committing other trespasses. When called upon for his defence he began to preach about the "tender Mercy of God," and to say that all men should be His followers and pray for mercy above justice, as justice and vengeance belonged to God alone and ought not to be practised by them that worship Him, and many other things till the Lord Chief Justice admonished Bedford for allowing him to speak in that strain. He then gave a formal assent to his guilt and said that he accounted it a small matter to answer to such a charge. He then began to preach and, being asked why judgment should not be pronounced against him, replied they had no judge among them as long as his liege lord, King Richard, was living in the Kingdom of Scotland. He was sentenced to be burned alive in St. Giles' in the Fields.

There can be no doubt but that this conspiracy was as much political as religious and was intended to destroy not only the hierarchy but the temporal power as we read in the "History of Leeds Castle," by Mr. Charles Wickham

Martin, that one John Longacre (otherwise John Wykeham of Swaylecliffe), formerly a mercer of London, was tried before Roos Hamlake and other justices for felonies committed in Middlesex and London since he and other so-called Lollards held diverse heretical opinions contrary and repugnant to the Catholic Law and the prelatical and royal dignity in seeking to destroy the King, his heir and brothers and the bishops and magnates of the land as well as reduce clerics, charged with the observance of religious and divine duties, to worldly occupations and to destroy cathedrals and other churches and relics and ecclesiastical goods.

Being sentenced to be hanged in the Fields, he was pardoned by a social act of the grace of God and the escheators of Middlesex were ordered to restore to him his goods to the value of ten marks.

The late Reverend Endall Tyler (late rector of that parish) quotes a letter written by Henry:

"I am informed by a man of considerable estate in England there hath been a man of the duke of Orleans in Scotland and accorded (corresponded) with the Duke of Albany that this summer he shall bring the mommet (impersonator of Richard) of Scotland to stir up what he may." ("Henry of Monmouth".)

And in the Pells Rolls we read:

"Also the escheators of the county of Kent, riding sometimes with twenty, sometimes with thirty, horsemen, for fear of the soldiers (disbanded from the army of France) and other malefactors obstinately favouring Sir John Oldcastle."

Sympathy with the unfortunate Richard was generally prevalent and the Countess of Oxford distributed badges of the "white hart" to "knights and valiant men". Among her followers were the Prior of St. Osyth's and the Abbots of Beleigh. The second sent his servant with his ring to Scotland and, when he returned with sure information that the late King still survived, declared that he would refresh with his goods and might.

In order to allay this rumour, Henry removed the body of Richard from the tomb in King's Langley to that which the late King had built over the remains of his consort, Anne, in Westminster Abbey with the effigies and adornments costing 400 marks and founded a perpetual memory one day a week on which six and eightpence was given to the poor and an anniversary when twenty pounds were distributed in pence.

On the death of that Princess, Richard had abandoned his palace at Shene which had fallen into ruins. Here Henry established a house dedicated to "the honour and glory and exaltation of the Name of Jesus most dear" for the Carthusians: and another at Isleworth to "the honour, praise and glory of the Trinity most high, of the Virgin Mary of the disciples and Apostles of God, of all the Saints, and especially of the most holy St. Bridget" commonly called Sion House for sixty sisters, thirteen priests, four deacons and eight lay brethren who wore woollen instead of linen cloth. The two convents has but one common chapel and both were endowed with the property of suppressed alien convents. At the Dissolution, the nuns fled to Zealand and then to Malines and finally to Lisbon where they remained till Wellington used their house as barracks after which they returned to England.

When the King was engaged in the French War, he was permitted to select his own confessor—a Dr. Walden known as the "Netter", since he was so skilful in combating the heretics—to officiate in his "chapel," which was furnished with altars and vestments and ministers, with permission to have the Mass celebrated at uncanonical hours and in interdicted places provided he were not the cause of the interdict. The doors were to be closed during Mass to exclude the excommunicated, and the services were to be sung without sound of bell and in a low voice and then very sparingly, especially before daybreak, as Christ was to be offered on the altar not in darkness but in the light.

In the last year of his reign he called together the heads of the Benedictine order to the number of sixty in the Chapter House at Westminster, being accompanied by only four persons among whom was the Bishop of Exeter. He contrasted the ancient piety of their predecessors and the devotion of the laity in endowing these houses and with the remissness with which they carried out their duties and their need for reformation, begging them to recover their former spirit and zeal and continue to pray for the welfare of their King, their country and the Church and assuring them that if they did so they need not fear their enemies. He advised them to pay attention to the cures of souls; to retrench their expenses and to abstain from riding about with more than twenty horsemen and alienating monastic property above the value of forty shillings; to be uniform in matters of habit, to relieve the poor in kind and not in money and to refrain from entertaining ladies in their private apartments.

A zealous churchman in the way of persecuting Lollards, he was not without compassion towards the dependents of those whom he had some reason to consider as his political enemies as we find in the Patent Rolls that although the goods of those who suffered were forfeited, "compassionating the poverty of Isabella Turner, Alice Young, Isabella Horewood and Matilda Finch whose husbands had been burned," he granted to them "of our especial grace" "all the goods and chattels to us forfeited for the maintenance of themselves and their children".

The campaign in France was successful, and his residence in the Louvre was crowded, while that of Charles at the Hotel de St. Pol was deserted and he married the daughter of the latter (Katherine de Valois) who was crowned at Westminster in 1421.

Being taken with his last illness at Vincennes, he exclaimed when he heard of the birth of his son at Windsor, "Henry of Monmouth hath lived a short time but had gained much and Henry of Windsor shall live long and lose much", and when, on his deathbed, the priest read the penitential psalms and came to the verse "build thou the walls of Jerusalem" he bade them pause and declared that had he been spared he would have proceeded to the Holy Land to free Jerusalem from the infidels and the MS. of Lille says that he had caused a survey of the coast of Egypt and Syria from Alexandria to Gallipoli to be made.

By his will he gave the charge of the young Prince and the kingdom to the Duke of Bedford, making the Earl of Warwick his preceptor in learning and in arms, urged both his brothers to be on friendly terms with each other and the Duke of Burgundy and not to release the Duke of Orleans.

But we must now turn our attention to the affairs of Church in the Catholic sense.

Alexander V only survived his election about twelve months and consequently had no chance of carrying out any reforms.

On his death the cardinals met in conclave at Bologna where, owing perhaps to bribery (for the cardinals of Gregory's creation were very poor) or intimidation (as he was in command of the papal troops), Cossa was elected and took the style of John XXIII. He held a council at Rome at which Wycliffe's doctrines were as a matter of course condemned; but, as Ladislaus entered Rome, he had to flee to Florence where he was coldly received as he had acted inimically towards Louis and had to make friends with Sigismund who had been crowned in 1414, and made him pay him the sum of

5,000 florins and promise to call a council at a certain place—meaning Constance, the seat of the most considerable See in Germany, embracing Baden and Wurttemberg and the lands of the Swiss Confederacy east of the Aare, except those districts which were in the dioceses of Como and Coire, and having within its bounds 350 monasteries and 1,700 benefices served by 17,000 priests.

John wished to go by way of Avignon in order to obtain the assistance of the French clergy; but the cardinals forced him to cross the Alps and he celebrated Mass before the emperor at Lodi.

The holding of this council was a great thing for Germany, as before this the Germans had but little dealings with civilised countries, unless we include the predatory incursions of the emperors in search of the crown imperial and various warlike expeditions in the north of Italy. Indeed the Southern Peninsula had been to them the "treasure house of the dwarfs" and the "graveyard of the Teutons".

During the sitting of the Council there were at one time or another something like four to five thousand strangers present, including two Popes, the Emperor, the Duke of Bavaria, the Margrave of Baden, the Burgrave of Nuremberg, the Count Palatine and sixteen other princes, one hundred and forty counts, seven patriarchs, twenty archbishops, ninety bishops, one hundred and twenty-four abbots, four thousand priests and sixty delegates of the universities. England was represented by the Earl of Warwick (who was allowed £330 for his expenses and those of his train of lords and gentlemen), Chicheley of Canterbury, Clifford of London, Hallam of Salisbury and the Bishops of Bath and Wells and "Chester" (Lichfield).

When the delegates were assembled it was found to be impossible to vote individually, and they were divided into Nations, each of which deliberated upon the several points and voted as one in the general assembly. In 1330, Bartholomew de Glanville had stated there were four Christian Nations, Rome, Constantinople, Italy and Spain; but the French insisted upon the number being reduced to three—France, Italy and Germany—the last including England, Poland and Scandinavia. This was contested by Hallam who said that while France only contained one hundred and eleven bishoprics with six thousand parishes, England was nearly eight hundred miles long (including Scotland, as Glasgow was in the diocese of York) and her Church embraced Wales, the Irish Kingdoms and the Orkneys, in which were spoken English, Cornish, Cymric and Erse.

As to competency, it was at first agreed that the voting should be confined to the bishops; but d'Ailly (Cardinal Bishop of Cambrai) obtained the inclusion of episcopal and capitular delegates on matters of doctrine and of princes in matters of discipline.

The emperor was unduly partial to the English and when he rode into the city he wore "the king's collar" (of the Garter) and invited the Lord of Chester (Lichfield), the Bishops of London, the Duke of "Bayer" and the "Borograve" of Nuremburg to dinner.

D'Ailly intended to welcome him from the presidential chair; but before he arrived Hallam was delivering an address and skilfully managed to retain his seat.

The proceedings were opened by the delegates of the University of Paris who declared that the council was assembled to discuss Church matters and stated that although the bonds between Christ and His Church were indissoluable, those between the Church and the Pope could be varied by the vote of an Œcumenical Council which was sovereign and could only be adjourned or dissolved by its own vote.

When, during the opening Mass, the deacon read as the lesson the words "And there went forth a decree from the Emperor Augustus", John turned pale; but was reassured when Sigismund took off his crown and kissed his feet, after which he declared his willingness to abdicate if his rivals would do the same, and suggested that the council should be adjourned to Nice to enable the emperor to negotiate with Benedict.

As this was taken as a desire to escape, he was committed to the charge of the patriarch of Antioch; but, he eluded his vigilance and fled in the guise of a layman with a crossbow slung across his back. Seeking to gain Avignon by way of Burgundy, he made his way to Schaffhouse (then under the influence of Austria) and the Council gave the Swiss Confederates to harry the lands of the Hapsburgs; but, he was captured at Freiburg and brought before the Council by which he was accused of leading an immoral life; of neglecting Divine Worship; of alienating the lands of the patrimony and goods of the Church; of selling pardons and indulgences, and of being a man of blood and carnal affections without any sense of honour, a mad man, a drunkard, a subverter of the Church and an accursed hypocrite; but the accusation of having poisoned Alexander was dropped. He was sentenced to lifelong imprisonment in Heidelburg Castle where he was served by peasants ignorant of anything save their uncouth dialect. Gregory had his act of abdication read out by Malatesta.

After having deposed John and accepted the abdication of Gregory, the Council was compelled to declare itself superior to any Pope and decreed that all questions of Faith should be referred to Councils; that two thirds majority should be necessary to secure any papal election and that, in the case of disputed elections, the decision should be given by the six representatives of each Nation —from this arose the practice of France, Austria and Germany claiming the right of veto—; that the reform of the Church should be left to the Sacred College and that no further council should be held till five years should have elapsed unless the state of the Church should necessitate one being called. As a matter of course the doctrines of Wycliffe were condemned and although his remains had been buried in his church at Lutterworth for one and twenty years, the Council ordered them to be disinterred and cast into the little river Swift. In spite of the safe conduct given by Sigismund to John Huss and Jerome of Prague, the Council condemned them to be burned outside the city.

It would seem that the work of the delegates was ended and they were about to disperse when the Bishop of Winchester (Beaufort) appeared and advised them to delay the question of reforms (which were to have been left to the Sacred College and the representatives of the Nations) and proceed with the election of Otto Colonna who took the title of Martin V in 1417.

CHAPTER EIGHT

CIVIL STRIFE AND THE COUNCIL OF BÂLE

Tribute to the Memory of Henry V—Court Factions—Marriage of Bedford and Gloucester—Jeanne d' Arc—Anarchy in England—Sorcery of the Duchess of Gloucester and Bolingbroke—Martin Attacks Chicheley—Ministry of Gloucester and Suffolk—Marriage of Henry—Death of Suffolk—Benefactions of Beaufort—Death of Chicheley—His Benefactions—All Souls' College and Higham Ferrers—Duke of Suffolk and Eveline—Molyneux Bishop of Chichester—Succeeded by Peacock—His Imprisonment—Clement VIII—Rome and Constantinople—Council at Pavia moved to Bâle—Council of Pope—Peace between West and East—Bessarion a Cardinal—Eugenius IV—Felix V—Nicholas V—End of Council—Madness of the King—Kemp and Bourchier at Canterbury—Battle of St. Albans and Northampton—Duke of York in the Lords.

THE Church of England was all powerful under the rule of Henry V. A MS. preserved in the college of Corpus Christus, at Oxford, states that Henry resembled Constantine, Marcian and Theodosvus as the preserver of the Church, which he prevented from sinking utterly by his remarkable piety and peaceful and mild government, which made for the safety of the Church and state by cutting off the heretical branches and casting aside of notable defects and abuses, some of which were caused by the excessive creation of cardinals to be supported by the revenues of the English Church and undue granting of indulgences and exemptions which encouraged the people in immorality, the ordination of candidates refused by the English episcopate, the evils of non-residence and the intrusion of non-English-speaking clergy into English benefices and prayed that all bishops who neglected the putting down of heresy should be deprived.

The first Parliament of the nine months old Henry VI met in 1422 and, disregarding the will of the late King, appointed Bedford as protector defender of the Church and realm and principal councillor of the realm, with a salary of 8,000 marks a year, giving Gloucester authority to act in his absence under a council and the Duke of Exeter and his brother, the cardinal, governors of the king's person.

The court was divided into two factions: one led by Bedford and the Duke of Somerset and his brother the cardinal who sought for peace and the other eager for war which was under the patronage of Gloucester, while the rest of the royal family, with Lord Dorset were devoid of influence.

The two leading politicians made unhappy marriages. Bedford had married a princess of the house of Burgundy and, after her death, Jacqueline, the daughter of the Count of St. Pol, whose petty state lay between France and Burgundy and whose policy wavered between those of his two neighbours.

Gloucester married Jacqueline, the heiress of Holland, Hainault and Zealand who on the death of her first husband (the Dauphin) had married the Duke of Brabant whom she disliked and from whom she was seeking a divorce from Martin. Failing to obtain it, she applied to Benedict and, fleeing to England, accepted an offer of marriage from Gloucester who raised an army, which was defeated, to restore her inheritance.

The war with France went on badly owing to the enthusiasm created by Jeanne d'Arc; but on the death of his father the French Council sent a deputation to congratulate the young King on his succession to the crowns, and he was crowned in Notre Dame in 1430.

Owing to the youth of the King and the intrigues of the Court England was in a bad state. The powerful families of the Percy's and Neville's were engaged in a private war in the north; and in Norfolk, after John Paston had obtained the judgment concerning the manor of Gresham in his favour against Lord Moleyns, the latter attacked his house in his absence and, besieging it with a thousand men, made his wife leave it by taking the beams away from the bedchambers.

The approaching renaissance was already showing gleams of light over the world. There is in every human mind a search after the unknown; and in the fifteenth century, there was a growth of what may be called witchcraft by which the ambitious minds sought to destroy their rivals and take their place.

Gloucester grew tired of the marriage by which he failed to obtain possession of the Netherlands and, leaving Jacqueline, married Eleanor Cobham "a sensually-minded woman" who had been his mistress for several years. A certain Roger Bolingbroke and Thomas South-well (Canon of St. Stephen's) were arrested for having laboured to obtain the death of the King by means of a waxen image and other acts of "negromancy," and having said Masses over certain instruments dedicated to carrying on their dark work—especially a painted chair wherein the first was wont to sit. On his being examined by Chicheley, Beaufort, Kemp of York and Ayscough (clerk to the council), Bolingbroke was condemned to hear a sermon by the Bishop of Rochester and to confess his practising in the Black Art contrary to the True Faith in the presence of the Bishops of Canterbury, London and Salisbury, and the Duchess of Gloucester fled to the Sanctuary at Westminster where she was examined by Chicheley, Kemp, Beaufort, Ayscough of Salisbury and others on a charge of sorcery, witchcraft, heresy and schism and sent in custody to Leeds Castle. All the defendants were then brought before the prelates and Lords Hunting-don, Stafford, Northumberland, Suffolk and Stanhope to be examined upon a charge of intending to do harm to the King and the Duchess was condemned to walk bareheaded and barefooted on three successive days through London to St. Paul's; and, on the third day, she was committed to the custody of Sir Thomas Stanley, who was assigned 100 marks a year to keep her whose "pride, false, coveteise and lecherie were the cause of her confusion" in safety.

During the lifetime of the fifth Henry, Chicheley had been comparatively free from the attacks of the papacy. He had shown himself an open foe to Lollardry and had passed many beneficial constitutions, such as preventing exorbitant stipends being paid to the clergy and moderating fees for induction and institutions, enjoining the celebration of festivals and allowing vicars to sue for their stipends in *forma pauperum*. He attacked the encroachments of the papacy and resisted the appointment of a perpetual legate, saying that as temporary ones had done much mischief permanent official would do more, and the English Church had no need of foreign buttresses. On the death of the king, Martin accused him of having neglected his pastoral duties and of only seeking to amass wealth, suffering his flock to browse upon poisonous herbs and, like a dumb dog, keeping silence while the wolves devoured his sheep. He then inveighed against the Statutes of Provisions and Praemunire as being against the laws of God and of man, as they allowed Jews, Turks and Infidels to land freely in England while his nuncios were treated as common enemies, and ordered Chicheley to use his influence to obtain their repeal under pain of excommunication. When his legatine power was suspended, he appealed to the judgment of a future council or failing that to the Tribunal of God. Martin then wrote to the bishops, pointing out the illegality of these Acts and sent letters annulling them to the primates and to the people of England. The prelates of York,

L

London, Durham and Lincoln, with the University of Oxford, wrote to Martin in his favour stating that he was like "the golden candlestick of the Church of England" and Chicheley sent a submissive later to his holiness; Martin ordered him to appear at Rome, as the nuncio had been imprisoned at the meeting of Parliament. The Primate with him of York and the Bishops of London, St. David's, Ely, Norwich and the Abbots of Westminster and Reading repaired to the House of Commons and advised them to yield to the papal demands but they wrote to the King begging him to obtain the Archbishop's pardon.

When Beaufort was entrusted as general of a Crusade against the Hussites and sought one tenth from all English benefices, all that Convocation would grant was eight pence in the mark should it meet with the King's approval; but, the nuncio thought this sum too little and, attempting to increase it, was imprisoned.

Bedford died in 1435, and his place was contested by the hotheaded and unscrupulous Gloucester and Lord Suffolk. When it came to a question of the King's marriage, the former would have married him to a daughter of the Count of Armagnac, the hereditary and bitter opponent of the French monarchy, but he had suffered a severe defeat that put the marriage out of the question. Suffolk following Bedford's policy of peace, arranged a marriage between the King and the beautiful, high-spirited and courageous Margaret, daughter of Reigner, Duke of Anjou, and titular King of Jerusalem, Naples and Sicily, who sought consolation for his lost kingdoms in patronising artists, poets and musicians in his poverty-stricken court. This marriage made the position of Suffolk secure for a time and destroyed the prestige of Gloucester, whose reputation had been damaged by the indiscretions of the Duchess.

Knowing that the Duke was in high favour in London,

the Parliament of 1447 was held at Bury, where he was arrested and died a few days later.

His death was followed by that of Cardinal Beaufort after an eventful life as a churchman, a politician and a warrior, who had completed the restoration of the nave of Winchester Cathedral commenced by William of Wykeham; another great memorial of him is the enlargement of the hospital of the Holy Cross at Winchester, founded by Henry de Blois, of Winchester, for thirteen poor men who were to reside within the walls and receive three quarterns of wheaten bread and a gallon and a half of beer. To this he added a dinner for a hundred men (poor citizens of Winchester) with leave to take home what was left of their repast and Beaufort increased the gift to provide one hundred more poor men, a master, a steward, four chaplains, thirteen clerks and seven choristers, who were educated in the establishment.

Chicheley died in 1443 at the estimated age of eighty. He also was noted for his benefactions especially All Souls' College, Oxford, for a warden and twenty scholars to study and to pray for the souls of kings Henry IV and V, the Duke of Clarence and all the dukes, earls, barons, knights and esquires and other nobles and subjects of these kings who had lost their lives in the French wars and all the faithful departed this life (on the site of Charleston Hall, Hereford Hall) and endowed it with lands of the suppressed alien houses of Abberbury, Woodney, Pinkney, Romney, St. Claire and Llangenith; but the greater part of the present income is derived from more recent purchases of land from private owners, especially the manor of Edgeware. As a foundation it was more lay than that of Wykeham as it had "sixteen jurists", "four artists", one chaplain and is at present confined to post-graduates and four undergraduates ("bible clerks"); while in New College there were seventy fellows, of whom twenty studied law and the rest (excluding the ten chaplains and three clerks) were to follow courses of theology, philosophy and arts.

Another foundation was a house for the education of Cistercian monks known as St. Bernard's College, which was dissolved in 1537 and given to Christchurch, by which it was sold to Sir Thomas White, who converted it into St. John's College in 1558. Besides these he founded two "hutches" for poor scholars, one of whom was to be a member of New College.

In 1442, he obtained a license in mortmain to purchase three acres of land in Higham Ferrers whereon to build a college for eight chaplains, four clerks (one to teach grammar and singing) and six choristers to pray for the souls of Henry IV and Mary de Bohun and Henry VI and Margaret of Anjou which he endowed with lands of the alien priory of East Mersey (belonging to St. Ouen of Rouen) valued at 300 marks. This foundation was enlarged by the aid of his two brothers who gave houses in London and the complete foundation included a bedehouse for twelve poor men. In 1535 it was valued at £200 and was granted to Robert Dacre on condition he maintained the school and almshouse and paid the schoolmaster £10 a year. Since then it came into the possession of the FitzWilliam family whose representative pays the £10 to the schoolmaster who has lost the house.

Chicheley was succeeded by John Stafford who was noted for his moderate views but we know but little about him.

The administration of Suffolk was far from successful and the great difficulty in England was that of finance. The King had made liberal grants to the greedy courtiers and had much diminished the royal revenue, being compelled to rely for his daily provision upon the exactions of the royal purveyors. The commons impeached Suffolk for maladministration and high treason. To the first he gave an excellent defence and recited his long service to the crown, but to avoid capital punishment he threw himself upon the mercy of the King who sentenced him to seven years' banishment. Leaving the country in a private ship he was captured by one belonging to the King and beheaded on the high seas. His body was washed ashore and buried in a college of his own foundation at Wingfield.

His Duchess (said to have been a daughter of Geoffrey Chaucer) was buried at Ewelme, where with her husband she had rebuilt the parish church and founded a "pretty hospital and almhouse"; being buried in the first under a tomb bearing her effigy in the robes of the Garter. She endowed the hospital for two priests "chaste of body and devout in soule" and thirteen poor men. One of the former was to be master and to instruct the bedesmen in sound doctrine and good life; the other was to be schoolmaster and teach the children of the duke's manors, each to receive £10 a year. One of the thirteen poor men to be the "minister" and present the faults of his fellows to the master and ring the bell for the "common service" with a salary of 16d. a week; the remainder only receiving 14d. This hospital was endowed with lands in the Duke's manors of Kenrugge, Cannock and Mershe which at the Dissolution were valued at £20 as "such large pennyworths were made to such as want to purchase".

The enthusiasm of the Lollards to a large extent died with the defeat of their leader—Oldcastle—the persecutions of Arundel and Chicheley and, except in the cloisters of the universities and among the minor parish priests and the peasantry in the remoter districts, they became a negligible quantity. The Church, in spite of her wealth, piety, learning and tradition of administration and statecraft had become feeble for want of spirituality and moral activity and was indifferent to giving that satisfaction to the people who were beginning to evince a spirit of inquiry that was the sign of the dawning of the Renaissance. The successors of Arundel and Chicheley were Stafford, Bourchier, Kemp, Russel and Rotherham who were mere politicians and more devoted to the successful dynasty than the Church.

We will now glance at the leading lights of the episcopacy. Adam de Molyneux (Mullins) was a member of a powerful family in Lancaster and became Clerk to the King's council, Archdeacon of Taunton, Prebendary of St. Paul's and Dean of St. Burian. After being sent to Rome to obtain the inclusion of the names of Alfred the Great and Osmund of Sarum in the calendar, he was made a full member of the council, in which capacity he attached himself to the party of Suffolk and was made Bishop of Chichester, with the rectory of Coddington *in commendam*, obtained exemption from the export duty on wool and from the admiralty droits for the seaborne parishes of his diocese and license to impark 12,000 acres and fortify twelve manor houses belonging to his See. Being sent to Portsmouth to pay the seamen their arrears of wages, he found them in a state of mutiny, and was accused of having acted treacherously in respect to the French war and of withholding part of the money due to them. Answering them haughtily, he was handled so grievously that he died within a few days.

The whole country was in a state of turmoil, and the people of Wiltshire plundered the chariot belonging to Bishop Ayscough of Salisbury of 10,000 marks and on the following Sunday dragged him from the high altar as he was celebrating Mass and beheaded him (still wearing the alb and stole) on the top of a hill.

Reginald Peacock was educated at Oriel and, through the influence of Gloucester, was presented to the mastership of Whittington's College and the rectory of St. Michael's in the Royal, provided to the See of St. Asaph's and, being opposed to Lollardry, wrote a book on the Christian Religion and in his "Donet" offered to withdraw all he had written or spoken contrary to the true doctrine. On the death of Molyneux, he was translated to Chichester (1450) to appease the clamour following the death of Gloucester. He was accused of having spoken against the extravagance of the preaching of the Friars whom he described as "pulpit brawlers" and severely censured by Archbishop Kemp. He inveighed against the meritorious efficacy of pilgrimages, the holding of landed property by clerks, the invocations to the saints and capital punishment and said that the clergy should find some better means of combating heresy than by threatening them with the gallows and the stake. In his tracts he showed that many of the complaints against the clergy were ill-founded and preached at St. Paul's Cross, defending the bishops from the charges of negligence and abstaining from preaching as to them is given the supervision of the Church. In 1449, he wrote the "Repressor" arguing against the idea that the Scriptures are the sole rule of human conduct as in many cases they are founded upon it. In his "Treatise on Faith", while not insisting upon the infallibility of the Church, he stated it were reasonable to believe opinions till they were found to be wrong and that neither Pope or Council could change one single article in the Creed as the Holy Scriptures were the sole guide to faith.

This angered the clergy as it appealed to individual judgment on the part of the laity, and several doctors undertook to refute his statements; but, the Bishops were loath to condemn one of their number and he would probably have escaped had he not been suspected of intriguing in favour of the Duke of York when they ordered his books to be examined; but when they contented themselves with condemning certain passages which denied the necessity of believing in the articles of the Creed relating to the Descent into Hell, and belief in the Holy Catholic Church, he defended the omission of the

first as it is not found in the earlier versions of the Creed
and that one should not believe in the Catholic and
Universal Church in the same manner that one believes
in God.

Being persuaded to recant, he was brought to St.
Paul's Cross where, in the presence of 200,000 people,
he acknowledged he had been a miserable sinner, trusting
in natural reason rather than the two Testaments and
the authority of Mother Church and had written many
heresies, advising the people not to believe his writings
and several of his books were burned in his presence.
Endeavouring to obtain restoration to his See, he was
proceeded against in Praemunire and imprisoned for
life in Thorney Abbey in the Isle, where he was deprived
of all writing materials and books save the Mass Book,
the Psalter and the Legends, with an allowance of £40
a year for his maintenance.

To return to the difficulties of the Papacy.

As we have seen Martin had proved to be a strong
Pope and obtained the submission of both Gregory and
John. On the death of Benedict XIII, the dissentient cardinals elected a Barcelona nobleman—Giles Munoz—
who took the style of Clement VIII (1429)—but he
resigned his position on being made Bishop of Majorca,
although two of the cardinals maintained the schism
without a head and without a following.

The eastern Empire, except the territory immediately
adjoining Constantinople, was in the hands of the Turks.
In 1353, the younger Andronicus had sent a message to
Benedict XII craving for aid, but no sooner had the
necessity passed than the quarrel between the East and
the West broke out again. Twenty years later John
Palaeologus again sought the protection of Urban and
acknowledged the Double Procession of the Holy Ghost
and the supremacy of the Pontiff.

When Martin had summoned a council to meet at

Pavia, owing to the outbreak of the plague, it was removed to Siena and Alphonso of Aragon sent an envoy to delay proceedings; and, it was again adjourned to Bâle but the Pope died immediately after it had been opened by Cardinal Cesarini.

His successor, Eugenius IV (1431) a Celestine monk who, as Cardinal Condelmero, had served the Church as treasurer and prothonotary, would have prevented the council doing anything.

Convocation had voted a tax of 2d. in the £ to defray the expenses of the English delegates, among whom were the Bishop and Prior of Norwich, the Bishop of Worcester, the Dean of Salisbury, the Chancellor and Precentor of Lincoln, the Abbot of Glastonbury and the Canonist de Desborough who were escorted by 150 chosen archers.

The war between France and Burgundy and the prevalence of heresy in Germany prevented the prompt arrival of the delegates who formed a council much more democratic than that of Constance as there were more proctors and delegates from monastic and capitular bodies than bishops and it has been called a "Council of Copyists, Scullions and Grooms". Instead of being divided into Nations, there were four Committees to deal with questions of Heresy, of the Hussites, of Faith and of Objects of Common Interest. Eugenius wished to delay proceedings till he could secure the support of the Orthodox Church and invited John Palaeologus to be present. When Amurath heard of this, he sent vases filled with silks and gold to Sigismund and the Germans were alarmed lest the emperor should adopt a Greek heir and so unite the East and the West. These negotiations occupied eight months and the assent of John was only obtained by the promise of 750,000 golden ducats for his expenses and those of his suite and 1,000 ducats or the services of 300 archers and galleys should Constantinople be attacked during his absence. Even then, he objected to go either to Bâle or Avignon as being beyond the Pillars of Hercules; but finally consented to go to Ferrara.

Accompanied by his brother Demetrius, Joseph the patriarch of Constantinople and those of Alexandria, Antioc hand Jerusalem and metropolitan Bessarion of Nicæa, Mark of Ephesus and those of Cyzicus and Nicodemia, the five Cross bearers of St. Sophia (who had no votes), Isadore primate of Russia and many scribes and philosophers, the emperor reached Venice and was conducted in great pomp to Ferrara.

During this delay, the council maintained the dogma arrived at at Constance that it was superior to the Pope and could only be adjourned or dissolved at his own will and summoned Eugenius to attend its meetings within sixty days. To this he foolishly replied by issuing a bull for its dissolution; but instead of obeying the doctors assembled said that the removal of the council would cause the laity to accuse the clergy of deferring all measures of reform and insisted upon continuing the sittings at Bâle, beat up laggards, held sessions to promulgate decrees, interfered with the government of the Venaissin, treated with the Hussites, sent embassies to various states and sought to limit the authority of Eugenius. The latter, harassed by the condottieri, had to grant concession after concession and to issue a bull recalling his decree of dissolution, while the council passed measures regulating papal elections, the celebration of Divine Service, the holding of diocesan synods, the abolition of reservations and presentation by Provisors and investigated suits between prelates, members of religious orders and holders of benefices.

On the opening of the council at Ferrara many Italians left Bâle, and there only remained thirty bishops and three hundred priests, the seats of the absent members being covered with relics from the altars; while, at

Ferrara, besides the imperial party, there were eight cardinals, two patriarchs, eight archbishops, forty-two bishops, forty-five abbots, representatives of the religious orders and many of the clergy.

The points to be settled were the supremacy of the Pope and the Double or Single Procession of the Holy Ghost. The first was admitted and the second was discussed from theological and legal points of view and at a private meeting the former doctrine was accepted on the emperor having promised to defray the expenses of his return, and that all pilgrim ships should call at the capital of the East on their way to the Holy Land and that ten galleys should be provided for the defence of the city; but above all Bessarion and Isodore should receive Red Hats.

The formal reconciliation took place in the cathedral at Florence, in 1439, when the Cardinals Julian and Bessarion celebrated Mass in Latin with the "Filioque" clause according to the Roman ritual.

Bessarion remained in the papal court as Cardinal and protector of the Greeks, served as legate in Bologna, Venice, France and Germany and is said to have been elected Pope but to have lost the tiara since his servant refused to admit the messengers from the conclave announcing his election lest his master should be disturbed in his studies: but it is unlikely that the Sacred College would have elected a Greek convert.

The council declared Eugenius schismatic, perjured, heretical and incapable of holding any office, ecclesiastical or secular, and proceeded to act as if the Holy See were vacant, electing Amadeus (1439) who had retired from his duchy of Savoy to the Convent of Ripaille where he lived in luxury amid charming surroundings. As Felix V his first step was to make himself Prince Bishop of Geneva, but the citizens refused to admit the member of the house of Savoy as prince. He was crowned in the abbey of St. Maurice in the Valais with a diadem said to have cost 30,000 golden crowns but was only recognised in his hereditary domains, a few imperial cities and parts of the Swiss Confederacy.

He is principally known as being the founder of the Order of the knights of St. Lazarus whose function was to succour the lepers in the Levant.

He ultimately resigned the papal dignity to Nicholas V. who allowed him to retain the style and habit of a pope and exercise the office of legate and vicar-general in Savoy and the Tarantaise.

Frederic II tired of the bickerings of Pope and council in 1447 ordered the burgomaster of Bâle to expel all foreigners from his city and the fathers adjourned to Lausanne (then Savoyard) where they held occasional meetings till the accession of Nicholas V.

On the death of Suffolk, the country fell into a sad state, the government being nominally in the hands of the King, but in reality in those of the Queen and the Duke of Somerset, a man of but little ability. As the King was still childless, an attempt was made in the house of Commons to settle the crown upon the Duke of York as heir; and in 1452 the last demanded the dismissal of Somerset.

The intellectual weakness of the King was varied by attacks of mania which perhaps inherited from his grandfather Charles V, caused him to rely too much upon those by whom he was surrounded especially the strong-minded Queen (who after the death of Suffolk) was influenced by Somerset and John Kemp (1380) who, educated at Merton College, had practised in the ecclesiastical courts (having been an assessor at the trial of Oldcastle), was Dean of the Arches and Chancellor of Normandy. Consecrated to Rochester at Rouen in 1410 and translated to London (1421), he supported Beaufort whom he succeeded as chancellor till he was translated to York.

In 1439 he was made a Prince of the Church and supported Suffolk in the negotiations concerning the French marriage; but quarrelled with him about the appointment of his nephew (Thomas Kempe) to London. He became primate of Canterbury in 1452; and, as the star of York arose, his visibly declined, and became more and more unpopular and was accused of neglecting his episcopal duties and being known as the "accursed cardinal", was only saved from disgrace by his death in 1455. A favourite with Henry, that King called him the "wisest of his Lords". He was succeeded at Canterbury by Thomas Bourchier, the son of the Count of Eu (and through his grandmother a descendant of Thomas of Woodstock, Duke of Gloucester, the youngest son of Edward I). Educated at Oxford he entered the Church and became successively Bishop of Worcester, Chancellor of Oxford, Bishop of Ely and Archbishop of Canterbury.

In 1454, Henry was seized with an attack of mania and the Duke of York was appointed regent; but, after the birth of the Prince of Wales (which destroyed the hopes the Duke of York had of succeeding to the crown), he recovered and released Somerset to whom he entrusted government. The Duke then raised his retainers, complained of maladministration and demanded reform in the state. Marching with the Duke of Norfolk and Lords Salisbury, Warwick, Devonshire and Cobham to the Welsh Marches where his influence was strongest, he returned to London only to find the gates closed against him. He then retreated to Kingston, whence he sent a letter by the hand of Bourchier (who entrusted it to two bishops) to the King at St. Albans; but, this was intercepted by Somerset and Thorpe. An encounter took place in which the King was wounded and Somerset, Northumberland, Stafford, Clifford and some 5,000 royalists were slain. Margaret took the place of Somerset in the King's Council and planned a reconciliation by which the new Duke of Somerset and Salisbury, Exeter and Warwick (followed by the King wearing his crown) and the Queen and York walked hand in hand down the nave of St. Paul's and swore a lasting peace.

It has been stated that the Wars of the Roses were between the upholders of the Parliamentary regime (as Henry of Bolingbroke had been selected by that body) and the upholders of the claim of the Duke of York by right of his descent from the Duke of Clarence (the second son of Edward III) but in reality it was the outcome of a weak, incapable government which aroused the antipathies of the rival nobles who were determined to settle their differences by an appeal to arms. The Duke of York was allied to the powerful Neville clan which had inherited the lands of the Beauchamps, the Montagues and the Mowbrays, boasted of five representatives in the House of Lords, were allied to the Percies, and had the goodwill of the great commercial centres which were against the bad financial policy of the Beauforts. Roughly speaking the districts of these parties were bounded by a line drawn from the Humber to Gloucester and thence by way of Bristol to Weymouth (but including a portion of the Marches of Wales). All to the north and east of this line was Yorkist and to the south and west Lancastrian. It was owing to this fact that these battles took the appearance of local and family encounters in which there was such fearful carnage as neither side sought or received quarter.

It would be useless to give any account of this terrible time during which the victory lay alternately with either party till Margaret was defeated at Northampton and had to take refuge in Scotland where she obtained the help of the Earl of Angus, to whom she promised all lands north of the Trent and an English dukedom, and engaged mercenaries by the bribe of the right to plunder England south of that river. It was with difficulty that

Henry—a prisoner in the Tower—was able to secure the freedom of St. Albans from plunder.

In 1483, the Earl of March (now Duke of York after his father's death at Wakefield) entered the Houses of Parliament and stood on the steps of the throne waiting to be invited to ascend it. When Bourchier asked the Duke if he had paid his respects to the King, he was told that he knew of no one to whom his respects were due and withdrew, leaving behind him a letter stating his claim to the throne. After this the Lords asked Henry who had the best right to the throne and received an answer that they and their fathers had sworn to obey his father and himself, but agreed to acknowledge the Duke as his successor which so angered the Queen that she made an offer to Lord Warwick that the Prince should marry his youngest daughter.

CHAPTER NINE

THE RENAISSANCE

Changes in England—Marriage of Edward IV—Rebellion—Eton and King's Colleges—Caxton—Tiptoft, a Product of the Renaissance—Death of Edward IV and V and accession of Richard III—Coronation—Battle of Bosworth and Accession of Henry VII—Acts against Liveries—Star Chamber Court—European Politics—Italian States—Spain—Marriage of Arthur and Catherine of Aragon—Her Poverty—Henry's Marriage Projects—Marriage of Henry—Duke of York—Henry VIIth's Chapel.

ENGLAND was in the melting pot and her social system was disorganised. The lay nobility had been decimated by the sanguinary character of the Civil War. No less than seven princes of the blood had been slain or executed at the battle of Towcester, where it is stated that the Lancastrians left no less than thirty-eight thousand on the field. Many who were spared by the slaughter by their fellows perished on the scaffold, and whole families had been ruined by acts of attainder and forfeiture, a proceeding that left the King owner of about one-sixth of the English soil. With the exception of the Poles, the Stanleys and the Howards (all of whom were of comparatively recent date but allied with the older houses by marriages) there was scarcely a powerful feudal family left and the middle-class, although rapidly rising into importance, was not sufficiently strong or well organised to take its place; and Edward IV thought of creating an official class of nobility which, with the Church, would throw in its lot with the crown and help him to found that personal monarchy which was overthrown by the Puritans.

He was astute enough to cause himself to be crowned by the fickle Bourchier who did not hesitate to perform the same ceremony for his brother Richard III (the supplanter of his son) and for the enemy of his house Henry VII; and, while seeming to dally with his courtiers, was evolving order out of chaos and building up his power by the acquisition of wealth to obtain which he used the ships of the navy to carry his merchandise to the ports of Italy and Greece.

The young king was only twenty years of age when he ascended the throne and Warwick was anxious for his alliance with the principal families of Europe. Among the matches proposed for him were those with the Princess Bona of Savoy: Margaret of Scotland (who had been betrothed to the late Prince Edward of Lancaster) and Isabella of Castile who was thought to be too young and afterward married Ferdinand of Aragon. When the Earl went to France to arrange for his marriage to a Princess, Edward went hunting to the Forest of Whittlesbury, and although he is said to have been betrothed to Elizabeth Lucy, he made overtures to the beautiful Elizabeth Woodville, daughter of Jacquetta of Luxemburg (Duchess of Bedford) by her second husband, Lord Rivers, and widow of Lord Gray who, being a Lancastrian, had suffered forfeiture. She made him understand that all overtures from him must be accompanied by a promise of marriage and the ceremony took place at Grafton privately without banns in the presence of the Duchess, two gentlewomen and a young man. Warwick was in France when he heard of this and of the marriage of the Princess Margaret to the Duke of Burgundy, the bitter foe of the King of France.

This incensed the Earl one of whose daughters had married the Prince Edward of Lancaster and the other the Duke of Clarence and he conspired with Margaret to place the Prince on the throne. Deserted by the

M

Neville-Montague and mistrustful of Clarence, Edward, after placing Elizabeth in sanctuary at Westminster, fled to Burgundy, and returning with an army the King defeated Warwick at Barnet and the Queen at Tewkesbury and by design or chance, Henry died in the Tower on the same day.

Henry had but little chance of benefiting the Church; but he was looked upon by the clergy as "blessed" and Henry VII sought to have his name inserted in the Calendar. He founded two colleges, the first at Eton for a provost, ten priests, four clerks, six choristers and twenty-five poor and indigent scholars (the number was increased to seventy) and seventy (afterwards thirteen) bedesmen. At Cambridge he built a college dedicated to St. Nicholas (King's College) for a provost, seventy fellows, ten priests, six clerks and sixteen choristers, endowed with lands of the suppressed alien monasteries.

Edward was a man of considerable culture and was the patron of William Caxton who had passed thirty years in the English House at Bruges during which time he had copied valuable MSS. for the Duchess of Burgundy "till his eye grew dim and his pen blunt" and he was glad to avail himself of the service of the printing press in the porch of St. Donat. Returning to England, he set up a press at the "Reed Pale" in the Sanctuary where he produced the "Commemoracions of Salisbury" and the "Golden Legend" for clerks; the poems of Gower and Lydgate for scholars, the "Eneydos" for knights and the "Legend of Fair Women" the "House of Fame" and the "Troilus and Cresside" for ladies. Among his patrons were the King, Lord Rivers and the "butcher Earl of Worcester Tiptoft" who was typical of the Italian Renaissance, but of a type unknown in England; a graduate of Paris, a learned lawyer who had translated Caesar and Cicero, written in Latin and English and impaled the captives of his sword, and yet Caxton wrote of him "there flowered in virtue and cunning none like him among the lords of the temporality in science and moral virtue."

Edward died in 1483 and left a widow, two sons: Edward and Richard, and a daughter, Elizabeth of York, with their mother at Ludlow. Lord Hastings persuaded her to let him take the youthful King to London and was attacked by the King's uncle—Richard of Gloucester—who took him in state to the Tower. The Queen then fled for the second time to the Sanctuary where she was waited upon by Rotherham of York and her brother, Lord Dorset, who weakened the position of the King by surrendering the great Seal and the Keys of the Tower.

Richard was aiming at the throne, obtained the surrender of his namesake—the Duke of York—on the plea that the Sanctuary was a harbour for criminals and not a fit home for little children, and held frequent council meetings to arrange for the coronation of the young King which he delayed from time to time to sound the lords as to the probability of his hopes of succession. He employed Dr. Shaa to attack the legitimacy of the late King and his son by preaching at St. Paul's Cross on the text "Spuria Vitulamini non agunt radices alta" (Bastard slips do not take deep root) and stating that the household of Richard Duke of York never recognised his son, Edward, as heir, but always looked to the Duke of Gloucester, and further that the late King had not been legally married to Elizabeth Woodville, as he had been betrothed to Elizabeth Lucy, and that marriage had been celebrated secretly without banns. He ended in fulsome laudation of Richard which, instead of being received with enthusiasm, was greeted with a volley of stones from which the protector and chaplain had to seek shelter. A few days afterwards the princes disappeared (1483).

Richard was ready to marry his niece (Elizabeth) whom his enemies desired to marry Henry Tudor (son of Margaret Beaufort, daughter of the Duke of Somerset) and to prevent the Queen taking her to the Continent posted a strong guard round the sanctuary till the Queen was compelled to surrender on the assurance of safety to life and limb and was committed to one Nesfield who was granted a pension of seven hundred marks "for the maintenance, exhibition and attendance upon dame Elizabeth Grey calling herself queen of England".

The Duke of Gloucester had married (1474) Anne Neville, Countess of Warwick (widow of the Lancastrian Prince of Wales) who had hidden her identity as a cook in the city and, being discovered, had been enrolled as an inhabitant of St. Martin's le Grand. An Act of Parliament of the next year contained the curious provision that the Duke was to continue in full possession of her property even if she divorced him on condition that he did his best to obtain a reconciliation and remarriage.

The coronation of the royal pair was conducted with great solemnity. They went from Whitehall to the King's Bench whence they walked barefooted to St. Edward's shrine, the King being preceded by the Duke of Norfolk bearing the crown, and the Queen, wearing a circlet of gold under a rich canopy and the Countess of Richmond bearing her train, following the Earl of Huntingdon with the sceptre, Viscount Lisle the rod with the dove and the Earl of Wiltshire the crown. After a service they left their chairs and put off their robes and "stood all naked from their waists upwards till the bishop had anointed them. They then resumed their robes and were crowned by the Archbishop Bourchier. On the death of their son, Edward, the King nominated the Earl of Lincoln (son of the Duke of Suffolk and Elizabeth, sister of Edward IV) as his heir.

Richard was very unpopular and the Duke of Bucking-

ham posed as a pretender to the throne; but, finding that
the antagonists of the King were in favour of the Earl
of Richmond (son of Owen Tudor and Margaret Beaufort)
whom Morton wished to marry the Princess Elizabeth
(daughter of Edward IV), conspired with him to provide
men to enforce his claim. The Earl brought a few men
to Poole, awaiting the Duke's land forces; but, as the
last were detained by floods, he retired and the Duke
was defeated and executed. In the following year he
landed at Milford Haven whence he marched to Bosworth
where Richard was slain. The battle was really one
between the immediate followers of Richard and Richmond, the men under the command of the Duke of
Norfolk and Lords Northumberland and Stanley remaining neutral. Henry Tudor, Earl of Richmond, had but
little trouble in establishing his position. His first act
was to offer the banners of St. George, of the Golden
Dragon and of the Dun Bull of the Mortimers in St.
Paul's. Parliament and the country at large were tired
of the continued strife of the rival parties and gladly
welcomed the event of a man who seemed strong enough
to maintain order; but the former would not acknowledge
his right by descent or by conquest and merely declared
that the crown "rested, remained and abided in him
and in the heirs of his body". Not wishing to acknowledge any claim through his enemies of the house of York,
he took care to be crowned before he married Elizabeth.
He secured the person of the young Earl of Warwick
(son of Clarence) and received the submission of the
Earl of Lincoln, who fled to the court of the Duchess
Margaret of Burgundy (who is said to have been the
most Yorkist of all her family) whence he returned with
an army of mercenaries to be slain at the battle of Stoke;
an engagement that ended the Wars of the Roses in 1487.

In order to break the military power of the territorial
magnates, Parliament passed two important acts; the

first of which forbade the services of large numbers of
retainers, most of whom were kinsmen more or less closely
connected with great lords and were devoted to their
chief and trained to the use of arms; and the other that
established the Court of Star Chamber. When Henry
paid a visit to the Earl of Oxford, the latter drew out
all his armed retainers and on being congratulated on
having such a large staff of domestics said they were not
servants but tenants; and as the King could not see the
laws broken so openly he fined his lordship £10,000.

The exact origin of the Star Chamber is uncertain.
As it played an important part in the struggles between
the King and Parliament, we will give some little account
of it.

In the twelfth century, the King's court was divided
into two parts—those of the King's Bench and the
Exchequer—and to the King's Council was entrusted
matters relating to the Jewish Shetar (bonds) as the
Hebrews were under the special protection of the King.
On their expulsion, the council assumed a permanent
form distinct from Parliament which tried to check its
authority. In 1341, it consisted of the Chancellor, Treasurer and Justices sitting in judgment in the *chambre des
étoiles* or "Camera Stellata", so called perhaps from its
being decorated with representations of the Seal of Solomon. Before 1455, Parliament had only recognised its
jurisdiction by acts of prohibition; but then an act
authorised the compelling power of its writs issued by the
Lord Privy Seal who, assisted by the chancellor, treasurer,
a bishop, one or two temporal lords and the two chief
justices, had cognisance of unlawful maintenance, granting of licenses, signs and tokens by the nobles, great riots,
unlawful assemblies, suits between great lords and cor-
porations and English and foreign merchants and other
causes over which the ordinary courts had no jurisdiction.
Towards the end of the reign of Henry VIII its powers

seemed to have reverted to the whole council and it had the power of giving to royal proclamations the force of law. It differed in procedure from the other courts and became the mouthpiece of the royal prerogative.

Henry was the first king who thought of making England a power in the comity of nations as in previous reigns foreign policy was mostly limited to the question of the rights of the English King to the crown of France or the privileges of the English merchants abroad. The central points of European unrest were Italy and Spain. It had always been the policy of Rome to prevent any monarch being powerful in the north and south at the same time.

The extravagance of the papal court and the cost of the papal wars had made the position of the papacy a difficult one and the peninsula was fast becoming the battlefield of the nations. The Venetians had encroached upon the papal territory; the King of France was seeking the sovereignty of the Milanese which was coveted by Maximilian and Spain was seeking the kingdom of Naples.

The rising power was that of Spain (shortly to be united with the Empire) and, with its immense wealth, its daughters were eagerly sought as brides by the reigning families and therefore sought corresponding advantages. When the Cortes of Castile deposed Don Enrico for his incapacity and licentiousness, it elected his sister Isabella as sovereign and her marriage with Ferdinand of Aragon formed the nucleus of a united Spain. The ambitious Henry sent Fox as an ambassador to solicit the hand of Catherine—daughter of Ferdinand and Isabella— as a wife of his eldest son Arthur. When he de- manded 1,000,000 crowns as a dower, the Spaniard minister Peubla thought it excessive and, considering that several of the King's predecessors had died violent deaths and that he was not secure upon the throne as long as there was a member of the Plantagenet family alive, was of the opinion that such a monarch should be content to receive such a daughter-in-law without a question of a dower; forgetting that Isabella came to the throne through a popular insurrection.

At last the negotiations were finished and it was agreed that the Spanish sovereigns should provide a marriage portion of 200,000 crowns and, in case of his death before ascending the throne, she should have one third of the revenues of the duchy of Cornwall and of the principality of Wales.

From 1498 she was styled the Princess of Wales and three years later was married to Prince Arthur; but, their married life was but a short one as he died in the following spring and was buried in Worcester Cathedral, where his mortuary cloth, emblazoned with the lion of England, the lilies of France, the pomegranates and castles of Spain with the figure of St. Catherine, can still be seen.

As a widow her lot was far from free from care and she was reduced to a certain degree of poverty as only one half of the dower had been paid, and from this £30,000 had been deducted on account of her wardrobe and jewels; the third part of her husband's income was withheld and he left his wearing apparel, jewels and plate to his sister Margaret of Scotland. As Henry was loath to repay the sum already paid and as Ferdinand was anxious to remain on friendly terms with England, it was suggested that the infanta should marry the second son—Henry—— On this point the council was divided. Warham, who had succeeded Deane at Canterbury, doubted the legality of such a marriage on account of the relationship; but Fox thought it would be expedient upon political grounds to prevent war between the two countries, although contrary to Church laws; and others of the council were anxious to prevent the money being returned to Spain and the Prince seemed to be agreeable.

In 1502, Elizabeth of York died and her husband, thinking of increasing the influence of his country, offered to marry the dowager Queen of Naples; but afterwards transferred his attentions to Joan of Castile, sister of Isabella who had died without heirs male. When he heard that Joan (with her husband Philip the Fair of Austria) was windbound at Weymouth on her way to take possession of the throne, he invited them to Windsor where he forced them to make a treaty with him for extending the English commerce with the Netherlands and surrender the Earl of Lincoln, promising his safety to life and limb; a condition he rigorously kept, although he directed his son to bring him to the block; besides this a clause was inserted for the marriage of their son Charles to the Princess Mary with a dower of 25,000 crowns. On the death of Philip, he was ready to unite the crowns of England and Castile by marrying Joan although she was a hopeless lunatic.

In spite of his overweening love of money, Henry spent some £140,000 in building the magnificent chapel at Westminster known by his name and left directions for fifteen hundred masses to be sung for the benefit of his soul in honour of the Blessed Trinity, two thousand five hundred in memory of the Five Wounds of Christ; the same number to the Five Joys of the Blessed Virgin Mary; five hundred and fifty in honour of the Five Orders of Angels; one hundred and fifty in honour of the Patriarchs; one hundred in honour of the Apostles and five hundred in honour of all the Saints, besides five hundred marks towards the furnishing of the Chapel.

CHAPTER TEN

DISSOLUTION

Great Men of the Period—Alcock of Ely—House of Lords—Character of Henry VIII—Julius II—Holy League—Wolsey, his limitation, plurali-ties and wealth—Alteration of Privilege of Clergy—Richard Hume—Francis I—Italy—Charles V—Leo X—Warham at Canterbury—Wolsey's Colleagues—Fate of his Agents—"Field of the Cloth of Gold"—Adrian IV—Clement VII—His Faults—Constable of Bourbon—Defeat of Francis—Sack of Rome—Wolsey Changes his politics—Heirs to Throne—Legitimacy of Mary—Question of Divorce—Court at Blackfriars—Catherine's Conduct—Wolsey's Household, his Fall—Reginald Pole, his Opinion of the Divorce—Cranmer—Verdict of the Foreign Universities on Divorce—Church in Praemunire—Affray of the Chauntry Priests—Cranmer at Canterbury—Reservation in Respect of Papal Obedience—Divorce pronounced—Marriage of Henry to Anne Boleyn—King Declared Deposed—Appointment of Bishops by *Congé d'élire*—Maid of Kent and Fisher—Sermon by Peto—Perilous State of the Monasteries—Execution of Fisher and More—Thomas Cromwell, his career, favourite with the King—Parliament Denies Papal Supremacy—Dissolution of the Monasteries—Adverse Verdicts—Arrest of Anne Boleyn and her Friends—Her Execution—Marriage of Henry with Jane Seymour—Act of Succession—Divisions of the Bishops—Cromwell and Aleceus in Convocation—"de Unitate Ecclesiæ"—Six Articles—Final Dissolution—Pilgrimage of Grace—Glastonbury—St. Thomas' Shrine—Cromwell and Audley—Impro-priate Rectories—Little Alteration in the Church.

THE Popes of the Renaissance were men of learning and artistic sense but as Churchmen they were far from perfect and their worldiness brought about the Reformation, and to make this clear we will give a short account of the successors of St. Peter.

Pius II (1458–64) who played a great part in the Council of Bâle, was opposed by Louis XI and Arch-bishop elected of Mayence (Diether)—of whom the first supported the theory of the sovereignty of the Councils and the latter exhibited an autocratic attitude in Church matters,—and tried in vain to unite Christendom in a Crusade, and, during the papacy of Sextus IV (1471–84), commenced the series of political Popes of which culminating point was the pontificate of Alexander VI (1492–1503) whose profligacy was notorious and who had to come to an understanding with Charles VIII.

In England the wealth of the Church was enormous. A traveller from Italy wrote in his *Relation* that out of 96,230 knights' fees no less than 28,015 belonged to ecclesiastics.

Education was almost entirely in her hands although a few laymen were beginning to take an interest in it, principally in the form of small schools attached to obits or chauntries. Alcock—Bishop of Ely—educated at Cambridge (M.A. 1461) became Dean of St. Stephen's, Master of the Rolls, and successively Bishop of Rochester and Ely, and obtained a license to convert the decayed nunnery of St. Rhadegunda into a college, dedicated to Jesus, for a master and six fellows; a number increased to eighteen and afterwards reduced to sixteen, of whom one half were selected from the northern and southern counties and six were to be in Holy Orders. He also built a chapel in Ely Cathedral, founded a school in Kingston-on-Hull, rebuilt the church of Westbury in Yorkshire and repaired that of St. Mary the Great at Cambridge.

Legislation was also in her hands; at the succession of Henry VII there were only eighty-two peers, of whom twenty-one were bishops, twenty-nine mitred abbots and three priors against twenty-seven lay peers. These were Jasper Tudor, Duke of Bedford William Fitzalan, Earl of Arundel and John Arundel, Lord Maltravers (both merged in the Dukedom of Norfolk); John de Vere (Earl of Oxford; Edward Grey (Earl of Kent); William Berkeley (Earl of Nottingham); Edward Stafford (Earl of Wiltshire); Richard Woodville (Earl Rivers); Thomas

Stanley (Earl of Derby); William Herbert (Earl of Huntingdon); Edward Courtney (Earl of Devon); Ralph Greystock (a barony merged into the earldom of Carlisle); Richard de Beauchamp; George Neville of Bergavenny; Reginal Grey; Richard de la Warre (represented by the Earl of that name); Thomas Lomley (represented by the Earl of Scarborough); John Broke of Cobham; John Blount of Montjoye; John Stourton (present barony of Stourton); John Sutton de Dudley (in abeyance); John Denham of Caredenham; Edward Grey; Viscount Lisle; John Grey de Powys; Henry Clifford (represented by the present barony); John Fitzwalter (represented by the present barony) and William Beaumont (represented by the present viscountess). Howard, Lord Surrey, was under attainder and Lord Northumberland was not summoned.

Henry VIII was a thorough Englishman, born and bred in this country; highly gifted; intelligent; well educated; astute and clever; he was a true son of the Renaissance and very popular; but these qualities were limited by his overweening love of display and self-indulgence in which he carried out the policy of Machiavelli who taught that monarchs were only bound by their interests and pleasure and not by the ordinary rules of honour and he sought to destroy all those who opposed him. Clergy, statesmen and wives alike fell under his displeasure when they had served his purpose.

He was not alone among brilliant men; his father, had with Louis XII and Maximilian, been termed one of the three Magi: in England he had as contemporaries Warham, Wolsey, Cranmer, More and Cromwell; and on the continent, Julius II, Leo X, Francis I, Ferdinand and Charles V.

Coming to the throne in 1509 at the age of nineteen, one of his first acts was to marry his brother's widow,

Catherine, in virtue of a bull of dispensation granted by Julius II in 1503.

This Pope was a thorough Italian, a warrior and a statesman rather than a Churchman, who was bent on restoring the prestige of the papacy against the powers of France, Germany and Venice. To this end he entered into an alliance at Cambrai with the Emperor, the Kings of France and Spain and the Duke of Burgundy, by means of which he made the proud republic withdraw to her seaborne limits and, after he had quarrelled with Louis about the duchy of Ferrara, the King summoned a council to meet at Pisa, a proceeding that gave him the opportunity to raise the cry of the "Church in danger" and to form the Holy League with Henry, Maximilian (who coveted the Milanese occupied by Louis as the heir of his grandmother Valentine de' Visconti), and Ferdinand who aimed at wresting Navarre from the French; all of whom looked upon the English King as a paymaster-general of Europe. The Spanish King provided ships for Henry to convey his troops to the south of France, assuring him of the ease with which he would conquer Guienne, but would not allow him to march to the East before he had pacified Navarre; and Lord Dorset had to return to England with a fever-stricken army. The next year, 25,000 English troops were landed in the North of France to aid the imperial army and the result was the capture of Tournai and Terrouaine.

Julius had seen the French driven out of Italy and, dying in 1513, was succeeded by Giovanni de' Medici, who as Leo X proved to be the greatest of the Renaissance Popes.

He quieted the Schism by which the French Church declared that she was bound by the decisions of the councils of Constance and Bâle and reconciled the various parties by the council held at the Lateran.

The leading churchman in England was Thomas Wolsey (1473-1530), the son of a wealthy grazier of Ipswich.

Going to Oxford, he was known as the Boy Bachelor, as he took his degree at the age of fifteen; becoming fellow and teacher in the grammar school of Magdalene College, he got into trouble for erecting the great tower of that college and acted as tutor to the sons of the Marquess of Dorset, who presented to him the benefice of Lymington, where it said that Sir Amyas a Powlet placed him in the stocks for drunkenness; a fact borne out by his confining the knight in his chambers in the Temple, but contradicted by his appointment as chaplain to Archbishop Deane and the governor of Calais. He rose rapidly in Church and State and became Dean of Lincoln and Lord Almoner. Being of obscure origin, he attached himself to the War Party led by the Earl of Surrey in opposition to Fox and Warham who were in favour of peace. He was the rival of Beket and Chicheley in matters of pluralities and, not content with the bishopric of Durham (which he exchanged for Winchester), Lincoln and York, obtained the Abbey of St. Albans *in commendam* and farmed the Sees of Worcester, Hereford, and Bath and Wells which were held by foreigners. In addition, he received large pensions from Maximilian and Francis and the republic of Venice which were not given as bribes but rather as retaining fees to watch over their interests in the Council Chamber.

In the days of the seventh Henry an Act was passed entailing the burning of the hand of all clerks convicted of felony which was modified by a subsequent Act, limiting this privilege to bishops, priests and deacons. When this was allowed to expire, the Abbot of Winchcombe supported it as being contrary to the laws of God and of the Church and declared that all who dissented from it were under the ban of the latter as all clerks (even those in minor orders) were sacred and exempt from the jurisdiction of secular courts. The Lords and Commons petitioned the King to repress the growing insolence of the clergy and he ordered a public debate to be held before himself and all the judges.

The case for the Temporal authority was championed by a Franciscan—Dr. Standish—who sought to prove that clerks had at all times been subject to that authority, as it was necessary for the peace of the Realm, and maintained that all offenders should be punished. This was denied by the abbot who said that holding such opinions was in itself a sin. Standish answered that no decree was binding till it had been accepted, and that clerical immunity as well as the compulsory residence of bishops within their dioceses had never been the rule in England. The judges said that he had the best of the argument and ordered the bishops to see that the abbot preached a recantation sermon which they refused to do as they were bound by oath to maintain the liberties of the Church.

About this time (1515) a city merchant—one Richard Hunne—sued by the priest of Whitechapel for payment for the use of a mortuary cloth before the legatine court, issued a writ in Praemunire as he claimed it was an illegal proceeding. Hearing that he was possessed of a copy of Wycliffe's *Preface to the Bible*, they (the priests) had him arrested as a heretic and, confessing the charge, he submitted himself to the mercy of the bishop. In the ordinary procedure he should have been sentenced to do penance and been liberated; instead of which he was imprisoned in the Lollards' tower of St. Paul's where he was found dead hanging by his girdle with his neck broken by an iron chain. The coroner's jury brought in a verdict of murder against the chancellor—Dr. Horsey— the bell-ringer and the sumner. The dead body was placed before the Bishops of London, Durham and Lincoln and charged with having possessed a copy of the *Preface*, and condemned as that of a heretic, and ordered to be burned. The three officials were indicted for murder but the Lords reversed the verdict and restored Hunne's children to the possessions of their father.

Convocation blamed Standish for this, but he pleaded the protection of the King who ordered him to hold yet another discussion and, when certain passages in his lectures on Divinity were alleged to be contrary to the liberties of the Church which the King was bound by his coronation oath to preserve, the Commons petitioned the King to extend his protection to the friar and he asked Dr. Voysey (afterwards of Exeter) to give his opinion on the question of immunity.

Another debate was ordered and Standish was accused of teaching that "the inferior orders of the Clergy were not sacred; that their exemption was not founded on Divine Right; that the laity could punish them and that the canons of the church were not binding till received, giving as an example the fact that celibacy binding upon the Catholic clergy was disregarded by the Orthodox Church." The judges gave it as their opinion that those who had prosecuted Hunne were guilty of Praemunire and the court broke up. In the presence of both houses, Wolsey said in the name of the clergy that, although they intended nothing against the royal prerogative, the trying of clerks seemed to infringe the liberties of the Church which both King and Parliament were bound by oath to maintain. Henry was satisfied by the answer of Standish who complained that a poor friar could do but little against the united Church. Warham said that many martyrs had suffered on that account and when the judges replied that many kings had maintained these laws and that many bishops had obeyed them, Warham desired that it might be referred to Rome. This was not granted and, as no evidence was brought against Horsey, he was acquitted, and it was said that the judges were more concerned to maintain their jurisdiction than to do justice; but the blame of the murder was laid upon the clergy.

In 1514 "Pope Juli" sent to the King a cap of maintainance and a sword by a great company of noblemen and gentlemen who presented it to him on a Sunday with great solemnity in St. Paul's Church.

Changes were taking place in European politics and in 1515 Louis XII was succeeded by the chivalrous and unscrupulous Francis I and Charles of Burgundy inherited the Crown of Spain in 1516.

The first was determined to win his spurs in the "graveyard of the Northern Nations" and assembling an army at Lyons, turned the flank of the Swiss mercenaries at Susa and poured his troops into the plain of Piedmont. At Marignano, he again defeated the Swiss in the fight called by Trevulzi "the battle of the Giants", after which he occupied Milan; but Henry, not inclined to go to war, contended himself with subsidising the Emperor and the Swiss.

Maximilian died in 1519 and Henry remembered the offer made to him two years previously of the crown imperial (in what manner it is difficult to know as the empire was elective); but, it seems that the tendency was to elect members of the House of Hapsburg and therefore Charles had a strong claim to the succession. Fearing a powerful antagonist with possessions on his south and east frontier, Francis put himself forward as a third candidate; but neither he or Henry stood the slightest chance of success and the latter threw all his influence on the side of Charles, who thus became master of Spain, the Netherlands, the Empire and the greater part of Italy with an estimated revenue of eighty millions of which two came from the Low Countries, half from Spain and the Indies, one from Naples and Sicily besides being master of the Mediterranean and the Spanish Main. As the King and Emperor were nearly equal in strength, they both sought the aid of Henry to maintain the balance.

N

Julius had died in 1513 and had been succeeded by Giovanni de' Medici (son of Lorenzo the Magnificent of Florence). Born in 1475, he was destined for the Church, and made a cardinal in 1489 with a proviso he was not to wear his insignia or execute his functions for three years. He had been carefully educated under the care of Poliziano, the philosopher, Mirandolo the theologian, Ficcino who tried to reconcile Platonism with Christianity and Sozzino the jurist. Opposed to the election of Alexander VI, on the expulsion of his family from Florence, he travelled in France, the Netherlands and Germany and, elected to the papacy, took the style of Leo X. His first step was to dissolve the schismatic council at Pisa, abolish the Pragmatic Sanction and hold a successful council in the Vatican. To protect Italy from the foreigner, he made a league with the Emperor and the King of Spain and, to ensure the friendship of England, made Wolsey a cardinal.

Bourchier had been succeeded at Canterbury by Deane (1502) who in his turn was succeeded by Warham in 1503. Educated at Winchester and New College, he became fellow of the latter in 1475, practised in the Court of Arches and served the King in diplomacy. Being made Master of the Rolls—a position he held for nine years—he was made Lord Keeper and Lord Chancellor which he resigned on being appointed to the primacy in 1503. In that position he was much troubled by Thomas Wolsey.

In order to gratify his pride, Wolsey sought to emulate Henry VII in building and Henry VI in educational matters and in 1528 obtained a bull from the Pope authorising him to suppress several (it is said forty) religious houses of good repute and hospitality; to found a college at Ipswich as a nursery for the noble foundation at Oxford (then known as Cardinals' College and afterwards as Christchurch). To do so, he employed several agents of whom two were engaged in a quarrel in which one was killed and the survivor was hanged; a third fell into a well and was drowned; a fourth from having been worth two hundred pounds a year was so reduced in circumstances that he had to beg his bread; a fifth was promoted to a See in Ireland where he was so roughly handled that he died; the Cardinal died of a broken heart and Cromwell on the scaffold. When the Prior of Daintree (sometimes spelt Daventry) refused to surrender a plot of land, he ruthlessly confiscated the whole of the priory estates.

Francis invited Henry to visit him but was forestalled by Charles who came to England and, being met at Canterbury by the King and Queen, was formally betrothed to Mary who was to be sent to be educated in Spain when she was six and married at the age of twelve.

The two kings met at Ardres, near Calais, where Wolsey celebrated Mass before them. Thence Henry went to the imperial town of Gravelines where they sketched out a plan for an alliance, and Wolsey gave his judgment against Francis for having invaded Navarre. The question of the marriage between Mary and Charles was ratified and the emperor promised to support Wolsey in the approaching papal election; but, in the end, obtained the tiara for his former tutor Adrian of Utrecht (1522), who only survived his election some twelve months, being succeeded by Clement VII.

Giulio de' Medici was the son of Giuliano and a certain Fioretta and nephew of Leo. In 1494, he went into exile with the rest of his family and, returning, was made Archbishop of Florence by Leo by a special dispensation on account of the supposed irregularity of the position of his father and mother; but this was followed by a declaration that they had been regularly married and that he was legitimate. In 1513, he was made legate of Bologna and during the reign of the pleasure-loving Leo proved to be a good administrator and his election in 1523 was hailed as the harbinger of a happy era; but, it was soon found that he was not able to act on his own behalf. His life appears to have been a blameless one and he was economical without being avaricious. A man of narrow views he was incapable of understanding the great spiritual movement within the Church and thought more of securing the interests of his house than listening to the necessities of the Reformation and, as his timidity prevented him from pursuing a definite policy, his pontificate was an unhappy one, as he always found himself on the losing side.

Among striking characters was the Constable Charles de Montpensier who, having married the daughter of the Duke of Bourbon, inherited his estates and assumed the title at the age of fifty. He had already seen much service in Italy against Maximilian and the Venetians; but his austere and taciturn manners offended the courtiers, and his wealth and military renown alarmed the King, who deprived him of the command of the vanguard in the expedition against the Imperialists. When his wife died without issue, Marie de Savoie urged the granddaughter of the Duke to claim the ducal fiefs, some of which she obtained while the greater part was escheated to the crown and he fled to Germany with a body of horse. Taking advantage of his discontent and anxious to avail themselves of his reputation as a general, Henry and Charles entered into a conspiracy with him to defeat the King of France and divide his domains; Charles to have Burgundy, Langue d'Oc, Champaigne and Picardy; the constable Provence, Dauphinée, Auvergne and the Bourbonnais as an independent principality, and Henry the remainder with the style of King of France; but little came of this as the English army retired after getting within sight of Paris, the constable fled to Germany where he was given the command of the imperial troops in Italy, with which he drove the French troops back to Marseilles which he was prevented from taking by the Marquess of Pesaro (who acted as a spy upon his movements), and Francis advanced to Pavia, where he was captured.

Henry promised to preserve the imperial rights in Milan and to invade France intending to meet the Emperor in Paris where he was to be crowned and then accompany him to Rome, where Clement was to reward the Emperor with the Imperial crown and marry Mary whose children were to unite the crowns of England, France and Spain; but the Emperor wanted something more substantial and made a treaty with the Queen Regent of France who promised to pay 1,800,000 crowns to Henry in half-yearly instalments of 50,000 each, an indemnity of 100,000 crowns to Wolsey for the loss of the bishopric of Tournay, and gave his two sons as hostages for the cession of Burgundy.

On his return to France, he declared his unwillingness to carry out this treaty and war broke out between him and Charles who sent an army of German lansquenets and Protestant mercenaries under the Constable de Bourbon who laid siege to Rome and, after his death during the assault, the city was given over to the sack by the infuriated soldiers.

Clement and his cardinals fled to St. Angelo whence he was liberated on the payment of 400,000 crowns and a promise to hold a council to deal with Lutheranism but on the eve of the payment he escaped to Orvieto and signed a treaty with the Emperor whom he crowned at Bologna in order to avoid holding the council at which he feared his legitimacy might be questioned.

When Wolsey heard of the imprisonment of the Pope he thought of being made viceregent of the papacy, with a seat at Avignon and control over the Church in England and France; but, when the Emperor became triumphant over the Pope, he changed his policy and turned from the imperial alliance as that of the enemies of the Church and allied himself with Francis.

Henry's only surviving child was the Princess Mary and the health of the Queen visibly declined. It was doubtful whether England would submit to a female sovereign and his nearest heir was his nephew (through Lady Margaret) James IV. His younger sister had married the Duke of Suffolk and had a son. Then came the descendants of the Duke of Clarence represented by the Countess of Salisbury and her children; and, lastly, those of Katherine (sister of Edward IV) whose heir was the Marquess of Exeter. Still farther remote was the Earl of Surrey, who claimed descent from the Duke of Gloucester, younger son of Edward IV.

About Easter (1527) the French ambassador (the Bishop of Tarbes) questioned the legitimacy of Mary, but Henry quieted Katherine by saying that any inquiry as to her marriage must end in its being declared without dispute, although she was aware that he was already smitten with the charms of Anne Boleyn. Wolsey spread about the report that the Queen intended to take vows of celibacy; but, the King stated that he considered her a woman of great qualities and that if he were free to marry again he would choose her above all others. When Wolsey and Campeggio announced to her that there was to be an inquiry about her marriage, she asked why no objection had been made during the twenty years concerning a marriage approved of by the wise King Henry and the affectionate King Ferdinand and divers wise and learned prelates, lords and councillors, and turning to the Cardinal, declared that he had acted thus because she had wondered at his vanity and vainglory and abhorred his presumption and tyranny and that he hated her nephew since he would not make him Pope by force.

Mr. Secretary Knight was sent to Rome to prepare Clement of the proposed proceedings, and he took with him dispatches to Gregory Casalli to obtain a commission

for Wolsey to act as judge and was promised a dissolution
of the marriage as soon as Clement was free from the
toils of the Emperor. Staphilius was in England and
was won over by the promise of a Cardinal's hat and an
English bishopric; while Gardiner and Fox were sent
with a draft of a decretal bull which provided for the
legitimacy of Mary.

Campeggio (Bishop of Salisbury) was joined with
Wolsey to act as a judge, and brought with him the desired
bull with instructions to retain possession of it. The envoy
besought the King to abandon his suit and the Queen
to enter a religious life, the Imperialists wished to have
the legates recalled, Campana was sent over to have
the bull destroyed; and Henry sent Brian and Vannes
to see whether if the King and Queen took religious
vows the marriage would be rendered invalid or whether
he could obtain a license to have two wives and the
Cardinal of England offered to provide the Pope with
the pay for 2,000 guards and procure the retrocession
of towns in hands of the Venetians.

When Clement became seriously ill and preparations
were made for holding a conclave, Wolsey sent directions
to Rome to secure the votes of the six uncertain Cardinals
and threatened that, if justice were not done, both
England and France would withdraw from the papal
obedience, and, at the same time, sought a reduction of
5,000 ducats for his translation from Durham to Winchester as the nominee to the former would pay 1,000.

The two legates assembled their court at Blackfriars
in 1529. Seated under a canopy of cloth of gold, they
received the royal parties, the King being represented
by two proctors and the Queen, only accompanied by
two bishops, made her obedience to the King and
besought compassion from him, maintaining that her
marriage was lawful as it had been agreed to by the wise
King Henry who, with her affectionate Father, was

considered one of the Magi of Europe and a second Solomon and, ignoring the cardinals as prejudiced judges, appealed to Rome. The legates received orders to draw out proceedings as long as possible.

Wolsey had reached the height of his power. Like Becket, he indulged in great magnificence, and his style was more regal than that of the King himself. Stow, in his Annales, gives an account of his household which it would be wearying to describe. His steward was always a priest, his treasurer was always a knight, his controller was always an esquire, and his coiffeur was always a doctor, marshals, yeomen, ushers, grooms and almoners, officers of the kitchens, the stables and a yeoman of the barge and of his chariot and of the garden. The dean of his chapel was a great divine; assisted by a subdean, a repeater of the choir, a gospeller, ten singing priests, a master of the children, seculars of the chapel, twelve singing men and the same number of children with a servant. At one time he had been seen in procession with forty-four copes of one colour with crosses and candlesticks, cross bearers and pillar bearers.

After the failure of trial before the legates in Blackfriars, his influence declined and, the Great Seal having been given to Sir Thomas Moore, he was indicted in Praemunire for having held legatine courts without the King's knowledge, to which he pleaded the royal indulgence as he had always acted in his interest if without his explicit orders. The only voice heard in his favour was that of his agent—Thomas Cromwell—and he was condemned to forfeiture.

Henry showed him great indulgence and restored to him the temporalities of York and Winchester and £6,000 in plate and goods, with orders to retire to York, where he was forbidden to exercise primatical functions. His progress to the north was an almost regal pageant. He was accompanied by one hundred and sixty horsemen with twelve carts bearing his household and three score wagons with necessities for his building. He lodged at first in the manor of the Abbot of Westminster at Hendon and, at Peterborough, kept his Maundy washing the feet of fifty-nine poor men, to each of whom he gave twelve pence (one receiving two shillings), three ells of canvas to make shoes, a cast of red herrings and three white ones. Arriving at Cawood, he made elaborate preparations for his enthronement which he had delayed for sixteen years; but, being suspected of corresponding with the Emperor, was arrested by Lord Northumberland, who would have conveyed him to London had he not died on his journey at Leicester.

Margaret Countess of Salisbury, the daughter of the Duke of Clarence of the Yorkish line, had several children by Sir Richard Pole, among whom were Reginald, the spoilt child of fortune. He had been educated at Sheen (in a school founded by Colet for the Carthusians) under Linacre and Latimer and took his degree at Oxford at the age of fifteen. Being appointed to a prebend in Salisbury and to the deaneries of Exeter and Shaftesbury, he was allowed to enjoy their emoluments while studying at Pavia in company of the aristocracy of the Renaissance; his colleagues being Contarini, Caraffa (both of whom were elected to the tiara), Bembo and Cadeleto (created cardinals). In 1525, he went to Rome and then returned to England, where Cromwell taught him that true statesmanship consisted in being in complete harmony with the chief of State who was not bound by the common rules of honesty or principles of honour. Henry sent him to Paris to obtain the opinion of the Sorbonne upon the marriage with Catherine; but he saw that Julius had not disposed of certain intricate points and that the more he studied the question the less he was able to form an opinion and spoke to his patron in no measured terms.

Although they did not agree, the King allowed him to retain the emoluments of the Deanery of Exeter and, on the disgrace of Wolsey, kept the Sees of York and Winchester open for his refusal for some time.

Another factor appeared upon the scene in the person of Thomas Cranmer (1489–1550) who had been educated at Jesus College (Cambridge) where he studied the Scriptures, the Fathers and the Records of the Councils. Ordained in 1523, he was incorporated in Cardinals' College as an M.A. and reader in Divinity. The turning point in his career was the meeting with Gardiner and Fox with whom he discussed the question of divorce, and recommended its being referred to the universities of Europe. This pleased Henry. At Oxford and Cambridge (after some hesitation as to the anti-Roman character of the affair) the majority decided that a marriage between a man and his brother's wife was against the laws of God and of nature. The universities of Bologna, Padua, Angers, Orleans and Toulouse were of the same opinion. After the Mass of the Holy Ghost and three weeks' study, the Sorbonne said that the Pope could not give a dispensing bull for such a marriage. Erasmus the man of peace—would give no opinion; but Bucer said that the law of Leviticus did not bind because God commanded them to marry their brother's wife, if he died childless; Zwingle and Oecolampdius thought that they were binding and that the issue of such a marriage was not illegitimate; Calvin thought that the marriage was null and that the Pope's dispensation was void; Melancthenon said that the law in Leviticus was dispensable, and that princes might make their own laws and the Venetian Senate refused to give an opinion until they were assured by the Pope that all canonists might give their views according to their consciences. And the Jewish doctors said that the marriage between such relations did not obtain out of Jewry.

Wolsey, Warham, four bishops, twenty-two abbots, forty-two peers and eleven commoners wrote to Clement complaining of the delay, notwithstanding the great merits of the King, the justness of his cause and its importance to the kingdom, and were answered by a complaint of the vehemence of their statements and the denial of any injustice, stating that he had done all he could and granted a commission but, as the Queen had appealed to Rome, the Cardinals considered that an avocation was necessary and therefore the blame for delay lay with the King.

The opinions of the universities were read in Latin and English before Parliament and Convocation and while the former showed that the King was not acting according to his own will and pleasure the latter, under the lash of Praemunire, declared that the marriage was illegal. The clergy pleaded that they had erred ignorantly, but were told that the statutes of Praemunire were still in force and nine bishops, fifty abbots and priors and the majority of the Lower House of Canterbury made their submission to the King whom they addressed as "protector and supreme head of the Church of England as far as permitted by the laws of Christ" and promised not to make any constitutions contrary to the authority of the Crown; adding to this a subsidy of £100,000.

The convocation of York was less amenable but in the end granted £18,000.

"The Clergie of England, being judged by the learned council to be in Premunire for maintaining the power legatine of the cardinal, were called by process into the King's bench to answer, wherefore in their convocation they concluded a submission, wherein they called the King the supreme head of the Church of England, according to the law of God and not otherwise, and were contented to give the King £100,000 to pardon their offences in Premunire."—ANNALES.

This sum was levied upon all the clergy.

"The chanterie Priests of London being called before the Bishop who would have had them contribute towards the payment of the £100,000 granted to the King for his pardon of the Premunire created such a stir in breaking into the Chapter where the Bishop sat that the Bishop was faine with faire wordes to dismiss them for the time; but after complaint made to the Lord Chancellor, divers of them and of their partakers were arrested and committed to prison to the number of fifteen Priests and five lay men, some to the Tower and some to the Fleete and to the prisons where they lay long after."—ANNALES.

To give the King a weapon against the Pope, Parliament granted him authority to withhold the "annates" (a tax upon Church land originally imposed to defray the costs of the Crusades but later forming a regular portion of the papal revenue) should he be pleased to exercise the right before the coming Easter.

Clement then ordered him to leave "one Anna" and live with his wife, and the King sent Dr. Bennet to Rome complaining that the Pope had been influenced by rash and ignorant men and could not expect him to be bound by a marriage condemned as unlawful by almost the whole of the wise men in the universities of England, France and Italy and said that he was unwilling to question the papal authority unless he were compelled to do so and even then he would do nothing more than to reduce it to its "ancient limits" and would not permit any change in the teaching of the "catholic Verities". This was followed by a citation to Rome in person or by proxy to answer the appeal made by the Queen which the King refused to obey as it would be contrary to canon law and prejudicial to the royal prerogative. The imperial Cardinals pressed the Pope to proceed to give an immediate judgment; but, the more moderate among them warned him that, if he pleased the King, the act against the collection of annates would not be enforced and that if he offended the King Parliament would side with the latter and it was likely that the King of France would join England in schism. The envoy then tried to win over the cardinal of Ravenna by promising him (in writing) the see of Ely or the first bishopric that should fall vacant, besides a benefice worth at least 60,000 ducats in France. As Ely was not vacant, and there was a question of suppressing certain monasteries to found bishoprics, it was suggested that the cardinal should be content with the income derived from Lichfield till Ely should become vacant.

Warham died in 1533 and they needed to find a successor. The bishops were but half subjects of the King as they were bound by oath to obey the Pope and also to obey the King and the clergy were bound by canonical oaths to obey the bishops who upon appointment the former had to sue out no less than eleven different bulls. The first confirmed the royal nomination and others required him to accept the office and freed him from all censure; others announced his nomination to the rest of the episcopal bench; to the dean and chapter or the prior (as the case may be); to the clergy of the diocese generally; to the laity and to the tenant of the episcopal lands; in the case of an archbishop, he was required to go to Rome to obtain the pall and another bull was issued to his colleague to invest him with it.

Henry fixed upon Cranmer as the new archbishop, and in answer to his "Nolo espiscopari" he simply replied, "Volo te episcopum esse". When he required the necessary bulls for his consecration, Clement sent them direct to Cranmer who forwarded them to the King and steadily refused to go to Rome; but was persuaded to send a proxy declaring that he should take the obligatory oaths to Clement "on the peril of his own soul". When he renewed these oaths at his recognition and consecration by the bishops of Lincoln, Exeter and St. Asaph, he caused his notary to record the fact that he took no responsibility for the taking of these vows by his proxy and reserved the right of acting in such a way as to do his duty to his God, his king and his country and of acting and speaking as his conscience bade him.

His first act was to hold a synod at Dunstable at which were present the bishops of London, Durham, Lincoln and Bath and Wells and many divines before which he summoned Catherine to appear but, as she ignored his jurisdiction, relying upon her appeal to Rome, he declared her to be contumacious and pronounced the sentence of her divorce from Henry, the notification of which he sent to her at Ampthill by a notary. Thence she was removed to Buckden (the manor house of the Bishop of Lincoln) and to Kimbolton where she died in 1636. Although she wished to be buried in the church of the Friars Observants, her body was interred in that of the abbey at Peterborough. She died in poverty and after begging the king to discharge her small debts, left money for 500 masses for her soul and directed that one of her servants should make a pilgrimage to the shrine of Our Lady of Walsingham distributing twenty nobles on her way.

The divorce was declared on May 23rd; but, already on January 25th, 1533, Henry had married Anne Boleyn (a member of a family long settled in Norfolk and related by marriage to the duke of that name) who had been maid of honour to Mary Queen of France (and afterwards Duchess of Suffolk) and Queen Catherine and is reported to have been affianced to Lord Percy, in an unfrequented garret in Whitehall by Dr. Rowland Lee in the presence of Norris and Heneage (the king's servants) and Anne Saville. At first, the priest demurred but he was reassured that the Pope had agreed upon the divorce and that the

King had a license for the second marriage in his posession.

This cutting short of the matrimonial knot that promised to be so fruitful to the Curia annoyed the imperialist cardinals and Clement posted notices as near England as Dunquerque requiring the King to restore matters to their former state under pain of excommunication and agreed with Francis that, if the King returned to the papal fold and referred his suit to a consistory (without the imperialist cardinals), a further hearing would be granted at Cambrai and judgment would be given in his favour; but the hostile cardinals objected to this as it would display to the world the vacillating mind of the Pope and demanded that his deposition should be placed in the hands of the Emperor.

Already (1534) Parliament, in which were present seven bishops and twelve abbots, asserted the King's supremacy and during the session ordered a sermon to be preached at St. Paul's every Sunday against that of the Pope; an Act was passed declaring that none could make any dispensation in respect to the laws of God, but that the King and Parliament could do so in respect to the laws of the land, and that all dispensations should be issued in the names of the archbishops and confirmed by the Lord Chancellor under the Great Seal and the King declared that he had not idea of altering any one article in the "very Catholic Faith". As many of the canons were found contrary to the law of England, a committee was appointed, consisting of sixteen laymen of either House and sixteen clergy to revise them and appeals to Rome were again prohibited but allowed from the Archbishops to the King as represented by a court of delegates appointed under the Great Seal. The method of appointing bishops was reformed by condemning all bulls and empowering the King, on a vacancy occuring, to send to the dean and chapter a *congé d'élire* accompanied by a letter missive securing the return of the royal nominee; after election the Bishop was to swear fealty after which the King was to issue a writ for his consecration and after performing homage for his temporalities, he was free to enter in upon his functions.

There was great opposition to the King's matrimonial schemes, of which we will mention two.

Bishop Fisher, Canon Bocking and Sir Thomas More were deceived by the ravings of a certain Elizabeth Barton—known as the Maid of Kent—who pretended to fall into trances during which she foretold that the King would die "a villain's death if he persisted in his wish to marry Anne Boleyn, within a month". Her imposition was discovered and she and her accomplices were hanged at Tyburn.

The Franciscan friar Peto, preaching at Greenwich, denounced the marriage in no measured terms, saying that those who encouraged the King in this respect were like the lying prophets who deceived the Hebrew king and that, if he persisted, the dogs would lick his blood as they had done that of Ahab. Henry listened patiently to him but ordered Dr. Corren to answer him in the same pulpit on the following Sunday. On that day Peto was absent but, after Corren had abused the friar as a dog, Friar Elstow said that Corren was like one of the lying prophets who would establish the succession to the crown through an adulterous marriage.

In 1489, Innocent VIII granted a commission to Archbishop Morton to inquire into the state of the Monasteries. He found that there was much to be desired in the way of reform and that the monks had relaxed their vows and neglected their devotions, contemplations and almsgiving and lived careless and often reprobate lives.

Their destruction was an expected thing and, when Bishop Fox, of Winchester, was meditating the foundation of a monastery, his colleague of Exeter (Oldham) advised him to reflect before he did so as the monks had already more than they could keep and he altered his plan and founded Corpus Christi College at Oxford.

This feeling was general and, in 1515, William Malby, an inhabitant of Beeleigh Abbey (perhaps a corrodier or pensioner), directed his executors to purchase a papal bull "under leede" (perhaps under the "Fisherman's seal") to enable the abbot or his "sacriste" to give 1,000 days' pardon to persons singing, hearing or assisting at the "Jesus Mass" in the chapel of that name and plenary indulgence to any one who should receive this pardon on Corpus Christi day and to grant the indulgence and pardon of St. John of Jerusalem to those who should kneel and say a "Pater noster" and an "Ave Maria" in that chapel for the souls of its founder and his wife and benefactors. He also gave 20 marks save 11s. and 1d. for masses for the souls of Richard Kirkeby and 8s. for those of his Lord and Lady of Essex. He also left his house in Maldon and another in Langford to his Aunt Katherine, "she doing no waste," for her life and afterwards to the Lady light in the abbey for 53 years "if the law will suffer it".

By an Act of Parliament all persons were compelled to take an oath acknowledging the divorce of Henry from Catherine and the legality of his marriage with Anne with succession to the children of the latter. More and Fisher, who had been pardoned for misprison of treason in the matter of Elizabeth Barton, refused to take it in its then present form as they believed if Parliament were against them in the first clause all Christendom was with them, and as to the second, Parliament had the power to settle the succession to the crown. Cranmer was anxious that their plea should be accepted as, if they swore to the last, the first was of but little importance. Both were committed to the Tower and when Paul II, unwisely sent a

o

cardinal's hat to the latter, Henry swore that he should have no head whereon to wear it and he followed the first to the scaffold.

Wolsey's place was taken by Thomas Cromwell, the son of a copyholder of Wimbledon, who rose to be a greater man than his master. He is supposed to have served in the French Army and, after the defeat at Gargliano in 1505, to have acted as a merchant in Florence. We next hear of him as a trader in Middleburgh and Antwerp whence he accompanied some traders from Kingston-on-Hull to Rome on matters relating to their trade guilds in 1510. Returning to England, he was elected as member of Parliament in which capacity he opposed the demand of Wolsey for a heavy subsidy and advocated that during the war with France, Henry should content himself with conducting the siege of Boulogne rather than risk his life and bring about a war of succession by leading his troops through that country. He soon attracted the attention of the King and became collector of the revenue, attaching himself to the cardinal whom he served in suppressing the monasteries in order to found his colleges. When Wolsey fell into disgrace, he rode post-haste to London "to make or to marr" and was the only one who lifted up his voice in his favour. When the Duke of Norfolk refused his services, he entered into those of the King whom he pleased by providing him with money and furthering his ambitious schemes and his upward course was rapid, even outstripping that of his late master, by providing him with money. In 1531, he was knighted, sworn of the Privy Council and made Keeper of the King's jewels and in the following year Clerk of the Hanaper, Chancellor of the Exchequer; then Master of the Rolls, principal secretary of state and chancellor of Cambridge.

In 1534 "Parliament began at Westminster, wherein the Pope with all his authority was cleane banished this realm and order taken that he was no more to be called Pope but Bishop of Rome and the King be taken and reputed Supreme Head of the Church of England, having full authority to reform all errors, heresies and abuses of the same. Also the firstfruits and tenths of all spiritual dignities and promotors were granted to the King."— ANNALES.

But Henry saw that the chief obstacle to his becoming the Supreme Head of the Church would lie in the monasteries which, being exempt from episcopal control and subject only to the Pope, formed a "Papal militia", and therefore ordered Cromwell to organise a general visitation of all religious houses and report upon their condition with a view to their suppression. Cromwell as chief visitor appointed his brother (Sir Richard) and doctors Apprice, Ley and Leyton to visit them and if possible to "put forth the religious persons that would go and all under the age of four and twenty years and close the residue that would remain so that they should nor come out of their places and took order that no man should come into the houses of women, nor any women into the houses of men but only to hear the services in the churches, and religious men that departed the abbot or prior to give them for their habit a priest's gown and forty shillings in money—the nuns to have such apparell as secular women should weare—to go where they would. They took out of the monasteries and nunneries their relics and jewels to the king's use it is said."—ANNALES.

The records of the findings of the visitors is preserved in the Black Book and Compendium Compertorium; but we must not rely too much upon them as the entries were often made to the prejudice of the houses.

The visitation commenced at Canterbury, where Cranmer preached a sermon, declaring that Rome instead of being the "Sedes Sancta of the Sanctissimus Papa" was the hotbed of unbridled lust and worldly pomp to which the prior replied with the words, "What a want of Christian charity!"

The visitors travelled all over England, and in certain cases obtained the surrender of the houses by threats, cajolery and persuasion. It is said that in cases they obtained proofs of the guilt of the nuns by violence, and wherever they went they caused a considerable amount of ill-feeling by appropriating the sacred vessels as drinking cups and the sacred vestments as saddle cloths and rugs.

In many cases they found a considerable amount of irregularity.

At St. Alban's the revenues scarcely paid for the expenses. The abbots had wasted the abbey lands, even the jewels had been abstracted from the shrine; copses, underwood and nearly all the forest trees (including oaks to the value of more than 8,000 marks) had been sold; the abbot dined alone at a high table (at the ends of which sat any illustrious guests) raised fifteen steps from the floor and was served by monks who halted at each fifth step and sang a hymn.

In the priory of Bray, the abbot had admitted a married women, living apart from her husband, as prioress. At Sopwell he changed the prioress at will and sent certain younger brethren to preside over the house as guardians who allowed its wealth to be dissipated.

At Fountains, the abbot wasted his substance in riotous living and had sold a large golden cross set with jewels and the same was the case at Mayden Bradley.

At Bristol the canons made much money by exhibiting the tunic of our Lord, a fragment of the Virgin's petticoat and the stone upon which Christ was born.

At Haleswell was a phial filled with the blood of Christ which liquefied when a suitable offering was made at the altar. At Bexley was a figure upon a crucifix that bowed under similar circumstances.

The record of the findings of the visitors is preserved in the "Black Book" or "Compendium Compertorium" but we must not rely too much upon the entries as the visitors that made their searches into the matters were inimical to the monks and were not impartial inquirers.

If we can trust the report, the abbot at Wigmore was an uncommon example of lax morality. He was accused of having paid the Pope 5,000 marks out of the common fund to purchase a bull constituting him a bishop (with the annexation of his abbey to the See) and of simony in taking money for avocation of benefice, besides selling Holy Orders to the number of sixty at a time to men who had been refused elsewhere in his private chapel or in another far away, at early morning or late evening, by which he made as much as a thousand pounds a year. He made a practice of selling corriodies, in one case to an old man and his wife, and when he heard he had made a will contrary to the interests of his house, prevented him from seeing his friends, broke open his hutch from which he took forty marks and deprived him of his feather bed. He defrauded the abbey tenants by enclosing woods and commons and by taking heavy fines for the renewal of leases, after which he would grant them to others on payments of larger sums and even alter the dates on the counterparts. He was accused of taking away a silver mantle from the image of Our Lady at Lentwarden and to have paid frequent visits to a woman at Welshpool whom he is said to have married.

But there were brighter spots. In 1524, Wolsey recommended the monks of the famous shrine at Glastonbury to elect the Schoolmaster and Chamberlain—Richard Whiting—a meek, gentle, courteous gentleman who made Sir Thomas More a corrodier with free "battels". He moved with the times and sought the good will of the greedy courtiers who longed for the abbey lands by concessions, manors and advowsons. He and his monks

accepted in silence the claims of the King to be Head of
the Church and under his rule a certain Renyngen was
appointed to sing and play the organ at Christmas and
teach six children to "pricke song and descaunte" and
to play the organ at the yearly salary of £10 and a robe
or thirteen and sixpence, two loads of wood and a house
or another thirteen and sixpence; the monastery providing "clavynge cordes". The vast abbey estates were
well managed and in the time of Whiting's predecessor
(Beere) there were at Doulting twenty servile families
(in reality thriving farmers) who refused to purchase
their freedom, and at the dissolution there were two
hundred and seventy serfs—perhaps the last that remained
on English soil.

At Woburn there were three states of opinion—the
abbot appears to have been in favour of the King's
Headship of the Church, but the monks were divided,
some wished things to remain as they were, others were
in favour of reformation and the greater number were
"indifferent". The first could have had their opponents
proceeded against as heretics, but, knowing they were
in correspondence with Cromwell's agents, contented
themselves with accusing their fellows of "heresy" and
"treason". When the order came to erase the name
of St. Thomas of Canterbury from the service books,
the officiating priest merely drew his pen through it,
saying he knew not when orders might come to restore it.

Catherine of Aragon died in 1536 and many thought
that, if Queen Anne's marriage were null, the King might
marry again in a more legal manner. The latter had
but few friends and there was much scandal as to the
way in which she treated the attendants about the court.

At a tournament held at Greenwich, it is said, that
when the queen dropped a handkerchief that was picked
up by her brother Lord Rochford, the King hastily left
the tribune and ordered five courtiers to be arrested and

the next day the Queen was sent to the Tower. The grand juries for Middlesex and Kent found a true bill for treason against the Queen and her brother (Lord Rochford); Henry Norris (groom of the stole), who said he would rather die a thousand deaths than accuse a woman whom he knew to be innocent; Sir Francis Weston; William Brotherton (gentleman of the Privy Chamber) and Mark Smeaton (a court musician, who signed an accusation against the Queen) were hanged. The Queen and her brother were tried before twenty-six lords presided over by her uncle, the Duke of Norfolk, (assisted by his son, Lord Surrey), among whom were her enemy, the Duke of Suffolk, and the King's natural son, the Duke of Richmond, who had married Norfolk's daughter. After Lord Rochford had been condemned (chiefly through the evidence of his wife), the Queen was brought forward and sentenced to be hanged or burnt at the King's pleasure. The day before her execution, she was taken to Lambeth to answer certain questions in respect to her marriage on "the salvation of her soul".

She appointed Doctors Wottom and Barber as her proctors who admitted her prenuptial contract with Lord Percy who declared on oath that although he had told Wolsey that he was so bound to her that he could not marry another woman he had entered into no legalities. Cranmer then pronounced her marriage with Henry as having been null and void from the beginning owing to her contract with Lord Percy.

The whole proceedings are wrapt in mystery as there is no record of the evidence against her and the "baga de secretis" only contains the indictment and precepts for her condemnation and, had the marriage been void, the charge of adultery falls to the ground.

The day after her execution, Henry married the beautiful Lady Jane Seymour, a member of an old family of

Wiltshire reputed to have been descended from the Duke of Clarence on the female side, who did not disdain to step into her late mistress's shoes.

Parliament then passed an Act of Succession confirming the attainder of Anne and the divorce of the two queens, declaring their children illegitimate and incapable of transmitting a claim to the throne and giving the succession to the children of the present and any subsequent queen or any person whom the King might nominate by letters patent or by will; and it was generally suspected that he would nominate his illegitimate son —the Duke of Richmond.

Paul, as Cardinal Farnese, had been friendly to Henry; but, after the execution of Fisher, he renewed the sentence of excommunication and the King replied by an act completely extinguishing the papal authority and declaring all bulls of privilege null and void unless they referred to marriages or consecrations and then they were required to be brought into chancery and confirmed and under the great seal.

As many of the clergy resided in the universities instead of in their cures, none over the age of forty except the heads of houses and readers were allowed to do so.

The episcopal bench was already divided into two parties those who desired things to remain as they were and those who wished for reform. The former were Lee of York, Stokesley of London, Tonstal of Durham, Longland of Lincoln, Voysey of Exeter, Clerk of Bath, Lee of Lichfield, Salcot of Bangor, Rugge of Norwich and Gardiner of Winchester who was abroad on the service of the Crown. On the side of reform were Cranmer, Goodrich of Ely, Shaxton of Salisbury, Fox of Hereford, Latimer of Worcester, Hilsey of Rochester, Barlow of St. David's, Barton of St. Asaph, and the uncertain Sampson of Chichester.

When the clergy met in convocation at St. Paul's, Stokesley sang the Mass of the Holy Ghost and Latimer preached the sermon, and, when they adjourned for business, they were shocked at the entry of Cromwell who although a layman had been appointed Vicar-General and as such took the presidential chair. Not only did he do so, but he introduced a Scotsman, Alesius, who had been obliged to leave his country for Germany whence he had returned with letters from Melanchthon to Henry who showed him such favour that he was known as the "King's scholar" and was living with Cranmer at Lambeth.

Cromwell opened proceedings by stating that the King desired that all controversial matter should be dropped and that harmony should be restored by agreeing that all points should be submitted to Divine Revelation. The King's discourse was censured and the Lower House complained of the sixty-seven doctrines that prevailed in England savouring of the opinions of the Old Lollards, of the new Reformers and of the Anabaptists which were merely indiscreet expressions flowing from the folly of rash zealots who would seek to throw discredit upon received doctrines and rites and which the bishops had been negligent in suppressing. Stokesley tried to prove by glosses and disjointed passages that there were seven Sacraments which was controverted by Alesius who maintained there were but two—Baptism and the Communion. This aroused the wrath of Stokesley who objected to the Scotsman driven from his country to seek hospitality in Germany daring to presume to teach the prelates of England but, Fox said that in Germany the Gospel had destroyed all the mysteries and fanatical rubbish of the priests and that the Germans had made the text of the Bible so plain that women and children wondered at the ignorance and falseness of the preceding years. The debate was concluded by the Bishop of London saying it was a mistake to think there be other word of God save that which a souter or cobbler could read in his own tongue, seeking to support tradition. The next day there was so much feeling against Alesius that Cranmer advised him to withdraw.

Pole was entrusted with a mission to bring about a General Council and, when to give him more authority Paul created him a cardinal, Tonstal said that for the vain glory of the red hat he was made the instrument to promote a rebellion in England. He wrote a voluminous book *de Unitate Ecclesiae* which was so virulent that Contarini advised the Pope to persuade him to tone it down as it attacked the King's supremacy saying that there was a great difference between the Ecclesiastical authority and the civil power; likening the people to the father of human society, the priest to the wife and the king to their son and went on to say that Henry, misled by ambition, had put himself up above the vicar of Christ and had made himself the head of a second Church which was schismatic and not Catholic. He thought that the people should show their indignation at the systematic plundering of Church property and declared that if Nero or Dominitian, or even Luther himself, were king of England, he would not have executed such men as More and Fisher. Knowing that Francis called him "amicus meus usque ad aras" and that as Charles was sweeping the Mediterranean clear of pirates, he urged the latter to change his course from Constantinople to England and attack the worst pirate of all—Henry—who had plundered the Church and reduced men's souls to slavery and that, while he had a divine commission to curse the King, he would hold his hand, and return good for evil.

This was answered by Gardiner who wrote the *Vera Obedientia* to which Bonner added a preface vehemently denying the Pope's power and asserting the King's supremacy.

Henry invited him to return to England and when he refused to put his head in the den of the lion, offered 10,000 crowns for his head. Francis refused to allow him to remain in his country and at Cambrai the imperial authorities treated him as a prisoner and his envoys were arrested at Valenciennes and sent back. His mother, Margaret of Salisbury, his brother, Lord Montague, the Marquis of Exeter (Courtney) and Sir Edward Neville were arrested. Cromwell persuaded Henry to make a league with the German reformers and the Elector of Saxony and the Landgrave of Hesse sent a deputation consisting of the vice-chancellor of Saxony (Burkhardt) George Boyneburg and Frederic Myconius (superintendant of the Church in Gotha) to London. They were welcomed by Cromwell and Cranmer and were badly lodged; but some of the bishops were more "noxious to them than were the rats that infested their lodging" and did their best to prevent any result being arrived at, as, while they were willing to separate from Rome, they leant towards the Orthodox Church. Cranmer thought he had convinced the weak Richard Sampson of Chichester but Stokesley won him over shortly afterwards by defending the essential practices of the Church which he said were found in the Greek Church, and the conference broke up without obtaining any result.

The two archbishops, sixteen bishops, forty abbots and priors and fifty of the Lower House signed five articles of belief:

1. That bishops and preachers should instruct the people in the Scriptures, the three Creeds, and the decisions of the first four general Councils;

2. That baptism was necessary for pardon of original sin and obtaining the Holy Ghost;

3. That penance, consisting of confession, contrition and amendment of life with works of charity; and a

lively faith and confession to a priest was necessary for salvation.

4. That the very Flesh and Blood of Christ were received in the Eucharist;

5. That justification was the remission of sin.

A. That it was good to have images in the churches, but they were not to be worshipped.

B. That saints were to be honoured but not to be expected to give those things that are given by God alone.

C. That the use of ceremonies such as wearing vestments, blessing holy water and holy bread, carrying of candles, palms and ashes, creeping to the cross and hallowing of fonts were good as they tended to raise the mind towards God.

D. That it was good to pray for departed souls and have masses and obsequies said for them; but as Scripture had not declared where they are or what they suffer the abuses of saying them in certain places should be done away with.

The visitation of the monasteries continued. Parliament granted to the King all religious houses having less than twelve inmates and an income of less than £200 a year as he needed money to continue the war with France, to put the kingdom in a proper state of defence, to improve the harbours and to strengthen the army and navy and gave him power to refound fifteen monasteries and sixteen nunneries with such rules as he might think fit, besides granting him the first fruits and annates.

Says Stow:—

"They took out of the manasteries and abbaies their relickes and Chiefest jewels, to the king's use. In a Parliament begunne in the moneth of Februarie, was granted to the king and his heires, all religious houses in the realme of England to the value of 2 hundred pound and under, with all landes and goods to them belonging.

The number of these houses then suppressed were 376 the value of their landes £32,000 pound and more by the year moveable goods were solde Robin hoodes penny worthes, amounted to more than one hundred thousand poundes and the religious persons that were in the saide houses were cleerely put out. Some went to other greater houses, some went abroad in the world. It was (saith mine author) a pitiful thing to hear the lamentations that the people of the country made for them; for there was great hospitality kept among them, and it is said that more than ten thousand persons, masters and servants had lost their livings by the putting down of these houses at that time."—ANNALES.

Stow appears to have underestimated the number of persons affected by the Dissolution and who appear to have been treated differently as the surrender was voluntary or forcible. In the first case, the abbots received pensions of as much as £100 and the monks those averaging from £10 to £6 13s. 4d., but in order to save these payments the first were often made bishops and the latter were presented to some unappropriated benefice. When the house was seized by attainder, no allowance was made to the dispossessed inmates and they were reduced to beggary for which they were liable to whipping and, on further prosecution, to multilation and even death.

The south of England was more amenable to the influence of the court; but in the north the dissolution did not pass off so quietly as the country was but sparsely inhabited and the travellers used the monasteries as inns in passing from one place to another, besides educating their children in them in hopes that, if they did not become monks, they might serve the houses as stewards and baliffs.

The first trouble broke out in Lincolnshire, where a priest disguised as a cobbler bade the people to be true to God, the King and the commonwealth, being willing to acknowledge the right of the crown to the first fruits and tenths; but complaining of the suppression of the religious houses. This was put down without much difficulty; but a more serious rising took place in Yorkshire where the insurgents were likely to receive assistance from the Scots. They were incited by fugitives from Lincolnshire, led by one Aske who organised them under the banner of the Five Wounds of Christ and made them swear to restore the Church, suppress heresy, preserve the King and his issue, and drive all baseborn councillors (such as Cromwell and Audley) from the court. Being some 80,000 strong they forced the Archbishop to recognise them and were joined by many of the great lords of the north except Lord Latimer who was persuaded by his wife (afterwards Queen Catherine Parr) to remain quiet. The Duke of Norfolk advanced as far as Doncaster and, as their numbers dwindled away, offered them a pardon with the exception of six persons mentioned by name and others whose name was not divulged; but, they demanded a general pardon, the establishment of a Council of the North modelled on the lines of the Star Chamber, a Parliament at York, the restoration of the Princess Mary to her rightful position, the restoration of papal authority and the re-establishment of the monasteries, the punishment of the visitors and the dismissal of Cromwell and Audley. The King replied that he would live and die in the Christian faith; but would not grant them a pardon while they were in arms and told them that, while he had four bishops and seven temporal lords in his council, the presence of Cromwell and Audley were necessary to supply him with legal knowledge and to correspond with foreign princes. Lords d'Arcy and Hussey and Carew were executed and many hundreds hanged. Several of the greater abbots were considered to be implicated in this attempt at rebellion and the commissioners hurried down to Glastonbury to find that Whiting had

removed the treasures of the abbey to his manor of
Sharpham. They suspected that he had secreted a large
amount of plate and coin, a quantity of money belonging
to the northern monasteries and compromising documents
"which we think to be very high and rank Treason".
He and the two treasurers (also monks) were hurried to
London where they were tried and sent back to be "tried
and *executed* at Wells". Wherein laid the treason is
uncertain as the hiding of money is not treason and it
belonged to the abbey until it had been dissolved, but,
there must have been something more to induce "as
worshipful a Jurie as was charged there theis many
yeres" to condemn him than mere transferring the
monastic plate from the abbey to the principal manor
house; or he may have been suspected to have been a
party to the abortive rising in the West. Being taken to
Glastonbury he and the two monks were drawn on
hurdles to the Tor Hill where they were hanged,
decapitated and cut into quarters which were sent to
Bridgwater, Ilchester, Wells and Bath while his head was
placed over his own gateway.

The Abbot of St. John's, Colchester, was indicted
upon an unknown charge. One of the counts against him
is said to have been that he said that the King should
never have his house but against his wish and against his
heart for he knew by his learning that he could take
it by law or by right. The Abbots of Reading, Whalley,
Jervaulx and Sawley and the Prior of Bridlington shared
the same fate.

Wrote Butler of Bullinger "the abbots are rotting on
the gibbets, a worthy recompense for their impostures".

The commissioners took possession of Glastonbury
Abbey which they despoiled of the lead and sent it to the
castle of Jersey, and, the monks and servants being
expelled, the place soon fell into disrepair as it was too
large for any one man to keep in order.

Dr. Layton had sneered at there being only two or three bachelors of Divinity in Glastonbury, but there was a large and valuable library there, containing the works of Pliny, Origen, Jerome, Anselm, Radulphus on Leviticus, notes on the Pauline epistles and the Gospels and books of the Old Testament, the works of Thomas Aquinas and Mauritius, Boethius, Virgil, Plato, Aristotle, Priscian, besides others on History, Astronomy, Geography and Music. Of these there can only be traced a list of relics, Bracton's *de Justicia* and, a perquisition book of Abbot Monington in the British Museum, and some Irish canons of the ninth century, and St. Dunstan on *Augustine* with a portrait of the Saint worshipping in the Bodleian.

Of the jewels we have but the mention of one—the great sapphire given by St. David which passed into the jewel house and may have been one of those pawned by Henrietta Maria or have been the stone given by Cardinal York to George III and lent by him to Lady Conyngham.

This monastery was one of the richest in England being valued at £35,000 (say £50,000 in the present currency) and was granted to Lord Hertford.

St. Austen's abbey at Canterbury was suppressed and the shrine and goods taken into the King's treasury. Also the shrine of Thomas Beket in the priory of Christ Church was likewise confiscated to the King's use. The shrine was "builded about a man's height, all of stone, then upwards of timber, within which was a chest of yron, containing the bones of Thomas Beket, skull and all, the woundes of his death and the piece out of his scull layde in the same wound. These bones by commaundement of the l. Cromwell were then and there brent. Ye timberwork of this shrine on the outside was covered with plates of gold damasked with gold wire which ground of gold was againe covered with jewels of gold, as rings cramped with gold wyer, into the sayde grounde of gold. Many of these rings having stones in them, brooches, angelles, images, precious stones and great perles, &c., the spoyle of which shrine in gold and precious stone filled two great chests of such weight as seven strong men coulde do no more than convey them out of the church. The monks were commaunded to change their habits into those of secular priests."— ANNALES.

The final suppression took place in 1539 and the 670 houses yielded lands to the value of £32,000 and movable goods to that of £100,000, but, the first amount (which to bring it to the present value of money must be multiplied by ten) was far below the real value as the convents were in the habit of letting their lands at a low value, making up the difference by exacting heavy fines on granting and renewing leases.

There appears to be some amount of uncertainty as to these figures and Tanner gives them as

			£	s.	d.
Greater Houses	186	..	104,919	13	4
Lesser Houses	374	..	33,479	13	7½
Preceptories of St. John	48	..	2,385	12	8
			140,784	19	7½

The money received through the voluntary surrenders was paid into the court for the augmentation of the Royal revenue and that received by forcible suppression and attainder was paid into the Exchequer.

In previous suppressions of alien monasteries and in that of Wolsey the moneys were either restored or devoted to educational purposes; but in this case, it was distinctly stated that the suppression took place to supply the King with money for the defence of the realm. Latimer and Cranmer wished to obtain the foundation of cathedral

P

schools to teach candidates for ordination and Divinity,
Latin, Greek and Hebrew; but Henry saw that if the
property were given back to the Church there would be
future danger of a counter Reformation and the restoration of the papal power. Sir Nicholas Bacon wished to
have a superior school for educating the sons of the
nobility and gentry in the classical languages and French
to serve the state as diplomats, legislators and chroniclers.
As the primary cause of the foundation of these houses
was to provide the celebration of masses for the souls of
the founders and their relatives and connections, their
heirs put forward claims for the restitution of the lands
and advowsons as being charitable gifts whose object
had failed through legislation; but many of these families
were extinct or had forfeited their rights through attainder. And then there were the courtiers who imagined that
the crown was in debt to them for services, and Sir
Thomas Eliot urged Cromwell to bring him to the King's
remembrance that in his boundless liberality he might
reward him for services to the state and Sir Humphrey
Stafford begged the powerful minister to help his "bedes-
man" to Warspring Abbey.

In Morant's "History of Essex" we find a long correspondence between Cromwell and Audley concerning the
rich priory of St. Osyth and the Abbey of St. John at
Colchester. The latter, a Colchester man, sent a true bill
of the contents of the Priory and said that he had not
received "eny penyworthe of the goodes". He had
already received from the abbot the manor of Abberton
(1538) and at the Dissolution begged that as he had "no
fee of office of his highness but the chauncelourshipp,
and although yt be hye and honourabill, yet yt is cum-
brous and chargeable" he begged that he might have
these houses given to him, and offered the Vicar-General
£20 "toward his paines".

Later he continued his request that the King should

transform the two places into colleges which would bring him in £2,000, with the gifts of the deaneries and prebendaries, as St. John's was in the king's town of Colchester "wherin dwell many pour people which have daily relefe of the house; another cause of these houses be in the end of the shire of Essex where litel hospitality shall be kept yf these be dissolved. For Seynt John's lakketh water and Seynt Oseyes stondeth in the mersches, not very wholsom, so that fewe of reputation, as I thinke will keep continual houses in eny of them, oonlez it be a congregation as there be now". To gain his end he offered Cromwell £200, beseeching him to "travayle therein, and advertise mwe as sone as ye shall se tyme of towardnes or ontowardnes thereof".

But Cromwell had marked out both these houses for himself and Audley had to be content with the rich abbey of Walden and the priory of the Holy Trinity in Aldgate, giving the latter towards the refounding of Buckingham College (Cambridge) as Magdalene College. Most of the real estate passed into lay hands and among the beneficiaries we may mention the Duke of Norfolk (although as a staunch catholic he was opposed to their Dissolution) the Duke of Suffolk, the Earl of Bedford, and Cromwell received no less than thirteen, thirty, three and seven each.

It is owing to the promiscuous granting of tythes to laymen and university institutions that many of the parochial cures are so poor. The wealthy abbey of St. Mary, at York, possessed many impropriated benefices among which was that of Kirlby Lonsdale valued at £1,300, of which £1,000 went to the Court of Augmentations and was afterwards given to Trinity College at Cambridge while £300 was considered sufficient for the vicar.

So thoroughly was the monastic tradition destroyed that there were few cases in which the church built by any of the foreign order (Cistercian, Carthusian or

Premonstratensian) is in use as a parochial church, and then it is because the church was used as such before its impropriation and then, frequently the monastic portion, aisle, chancel, or transept have been destroyed. The inhabitants of St. Albans had used the nave of the abbey church for generations and at the Dissolution retained their right to it; at St. Helen's (Bishopsgate) the nuns' nave was united to that of the parish and at Tewkesbury the inhabitants purchased the exclusively monastic portions from the commissioners at the price of £4,000. At Bath, the inhabitants refused the offer of the roofless abbey church till it was presented to them by Matthew Colthurst in 1560.

There was but little change in doctrine except the name of the Pope and of St. Thomas of Canterbury were omitted from the calendar and as a rule the personnel of the church remained as it was and the principal alteration was that in the monastic churches converted into cathedrals the bishop lost his position as abbot; the prior became dean and the monks canons, precentors and choristers and received their portion of the monastic estates till the Great Spoliation. Some of the monastic churches were made collegiate such as those at St. Albans, Truro, Liverpool, Ripon, Manchester, Newcastle, Southwell, Windsor, Heytesbury, Middleham and Wolverhampton, of which several have been made cathedrals and others dissolved by the Ecclesiastical Commissioners.

" They tell us that the Lord of Host will not avenge His
    own,
  They tell us that He careth not for temples overthrown;
  Go! Look through England's thousand vales, and show
    me, he that may,
  The abbey lands that have not wrought their owners'
    swift decay."

—Dr. J. Mason Neale.

CHAPTER ELEVEN

REFORMATION

THE destruction of the monastic system and the ruthless
way in which Henry visited any infringement of his
prerogative crippled the power of Rome and left England
in an uncertain state as to religion, and the progress
towards the Reformation was slow as the King was still
attached to the "Verity of the Catholic Faith" as under-
stood by himself. In fact there was but little advance
in this direction during his reign.

The German Protestant princes negotiated with the
King, insisting upon the granting of the chalice to the
laity, putting down the private masses, worshipping in
the vernacular and abolishing the celibacy of the clergy.
In 1539, Parliament met and there were present twenty
abbots, Cranmer, the bishops of Durham, Ely, Bath and
Wells, Bangor, Carlisle and Worcester and the Duke of
Norfolk, who was the head of the Romanist party.
These were divided, but eventually agreed upon six

Articles enjoining the Corporal presence, the observance of vows of chastity, the continuance of private masses, the celibacy of the clergy and auricular confession. These were supplemented by an act of Parliament which provided for the penalty of death against any one disputing the first article and the declaration of felony for speaking against the rest. The retention of wives by the priests involved a Praemunire for the first offence and felony for the second, and the wives incurred the same penalty as their husbands, and all priests were ordered to read the statute from their pulpits once every quarter.

The Bishops of Canterbury, Worcester, Rochester, St. David's and Salisbury were opposed to this Act, Cranmer sent his wife (the niece of Osiander) abroad and Latimer laid down his bishopric and withdrew into the country; but, falling from his horse, had to come to London for surgical assistance, was arrested and remained in the Tower till the King's death, and Shaxton also resigned his see.

This was followed by an act to enable the King to establish fresh bishoprics and the places selected were:

1. Waltham for Essex;
2. St. Albans for Hertfordshire;
3. One for Bedfordshire and Buckinghamshire, out of of the monasteries of Dunstable, Newnham and Clowestow;
4. Another for Oxfordshire and Berkshire out of the rents of Oseney and Thane;
5. One for Northamptonshire and Huntingdonshire out of the estates of Peterborough;
6. One for Middlesex (except the archiepiscopal manor of Fulham) out of the property of Westminster Abbey;
7. One for Rutlandshire and Leicester out of the Abbey in the latter place;
8. One for Gloucester out of St. Peter's Abbey.

9. One for Lancaster out of Fountains and the arch-deaconry of Richmondshire;
10. One for Suffolk out of Bury Abbey;
11. One for Staffordshire and Shropshire out of Shrewsbury Abbey;
12. One for Nottingham and Derby out of Welbeck, Worksop and Thurgarton;
13. One for Cornwall out of the rents of Launceston, Bodmin and Wardeth.

NOTE

The Rev. Mackenzie Walcott gives in the "Transactions of the Essex Archaeological Society" the following details of the endowment of the See of Waltham.

A bishop or president 23£ 6s. 8d. (for the corps of his promotion 9£ and 6d. by day);

5 Prebendaries each by the year 20£ 9s. (the corps 7£ and 8s. by day) a reader in Divinity 20£;

4 Petty canons to sing (MS. B to keep the quire in the quire) each 8s—1£. In MS. B there are six, one to be a sexton.

A Gospeller 6£, a Pysteller 100s. (in MS. B like the petty canons they were to have 1£);

6 Laymen to sing and serve in the quire each 6£ 13s. 4d.;

8 choristers each 5 marks: Master of the children 3£ 13s. 4d.;

4 students of Divinity at Oxford and at Cambridge each 40£ and 20 scholars 5 marks.

—Vol V. 264.

Parliament confirmed the sentences passed upon the Marquis of Exeter (upon the slight grounds of his being suspected of complicity in the revolt in the West) and Lord Montacute and passed a bill of attainder against the Countess of Salisbury on the slender evidence of having in her possession a vestment embroidered with the Five Wounds, the Sacred Monogram, the Host and and the Plantagenet Arms, alleged to be a sign that the Pilgrimage of Grace was planned to place her son, the Cardinal, on the throne. At first the Lords were doubtful whether they could judge an absent person; but Cromwell invited the judges to his house and obtained their opinion that, as they were the highest court, they could not be called to account for their action. The Countess languished in the Tower for some time and was beheaded in 1541.

Cromwell was anxious to unite the German Protestants with the English Reformers. The King had remained a widower for three years after the death of Lady Jane Seymour and thought of marrying Christina, the Dowager Duchess of Milan (niece of the Emperor), who, hearing of his offer, lamented that she had only one neck or she would place the second at his service. Had this marriage taken place it would have made a great difference to the Reformation since, as she was a kinswoman of Catherine of Aragon, it would have been necessary to obtain a dispensing bull from Paul who made it a previous condition that Henry should become reconciled to Rome. Another lady was Marie of Lorraine, betrothed to the King of Scotland, and, failing her, Mdlle. de Vendome; but when the King requested Francis to allow his agent to select the fairest dame in France, he refused to allow them to be trotted out like horses for inspection. Other matrimonial projects was a marriage with the Infanta of Portugal and that of Edward to the youngest daughter of the emperor, the Ladies Mary to an infant of Portugal and Elizabeth to the King of Hungary.

But Cromwell fixed upon the Lady Anne of Cleves, the sister of the brilliant and beautiful Electress of Saxony, and employed Holbein to produce a flattering portrait of her that pleased the King; but meeting her at Rochester, he took a dislike to her and obtained a decree of nullity of marriage on the grounds of her having been betrothed to the Prince of Lorraine. She was only too pleased at escaping with her life, and gladly accepted the style of the King's sister with precedence over all the ladies of the court (except Mary and Elizabeth), a pension of £3,000 a year and a residence at Richmond.

In 1527, William Tyndale had completed a translation of the Bible from the Hebrew and Greek into English for which there was a large demand, and the clergy were alarmed at the circulation of a "new book" taken from a "newly found language called Greek" in which there were "many pitfalls, hard sayings and dark sentences, and briars and thorns of heresies." Had he been content with publishing the text, the opposition might have disappeared, but he inserted many anti-papal notes and incurred the undying hatred of the King by his opposition to his divorce from Catherine.

In 1530, Convocation, seeing that they could not prevent the circulation of the Scriptures in England, petitioned the King to set forth an authorised Version, but he said he would wait until there was more concord and agreement between learned and Catholic men and the project was dropped for four years when Cranmer proposed to Convocation that the work should be undertaken by certain honourable and learned men to be circulated among the people. This was objected to by Stokesley and Gardiner, who said that the teaching of the Church was sufficient without bringing in Tyndale's New Testament and heretical books from beyond the seas, but, in 1534 the Archbishop laid the proposal before the King with the proviso that the translation should be circulated among the people, according to their knowledge, and all books suspected of heresy should be delivered up. He accordingly distributed ten portions of the New Testament, probably the work of Tyndale, among the bishops asking them to return them by a certain date with their remarks. This was done, with the exception of the Acts of the Apostles concerning which, Stokesley said, he would not give an hour to a task that would plunge the people into heresy.

Tyndale was languishing in prison at Vilvorde, having been charged with declaring that Faith alone justifies in his tract "The Unjust Mammon" which appeared in London under the title "Treatise of Justification through Faith". After having been degraded, he endured much suffering in his cell and was burned on October 6th, 1536.

It is generally supposed that Tyndale gave his MSS. to John Rogers, chaplain of the English Company at Antwerp, who may have revised them. Anyhow a Bible somewhat similar to that of the martyr was shown to Grafton and gained his approval. It was submitted to Cromwell first, and Cranmer, who is said to have largely contributed £500 to its production, said he would rather see it licensed by the King than receive £1,000, and thought that "if they waited till the bishops should set forth a better translation they might wait till doomsday". The King, seeing that Tyndale's name was not on the title page, freely gave his consent.

Stow writes:

"This moneth (September 1536) Thomas, Dr. Barnes, Garret (curate of Honey Lane) and Jerome (vicar of Stepney)—the last two having belonged to the Christian Brotherhood pledged to promote the circulation of Tyndale's New Testament, here ordered to preach at St. Paul's."

Bishop Bonner claimed the right to preach the first sermon, and selected the text "Cast thyself down", saying that nowadays there was nothing forward in the Church as the devil taught men "come back from fasting, come back from praying, come back from confession and come back from weeping for sin and soon the people will say the Paternoster backward"; and that, as it was formerly said that Heaven was sold at Rome for a little money, now the devil offers it for nothing. On the following Sunday, Barnes preached before him and the Lord Mayor and made the mistake of punning upon the name of the Bishop of Winchester, complaining that the "gardener had neglected to take the tares from the garden of the Lord". He was followed by Garret who gave no cause for complaint; but Jerome preached from the Galatians saying that all who are born of Sarah—that is are regenerated in Faith—are fully and positively justified.

Henry then ordered them to preach recanting sermons at St. Mary Spital, and Barnes obeyed by apologising to Gardiner but continued by preaching the Gospel doctrine of Salvation by Grace. The three were committed to the Tower where three Papists, Abel (the friend of Catherine of Aragon), Featherstone and Powel were in confinement for denying the King's Supremacy. In order to show no partiality, Barnes and Abel, Garret and Featherstone and Jerome and Powel were tied to three hurdles and dragged to Smithfield where the Catholics were hanged and the Reformers burned.

A foreign spectator is said to have exclaimed "Here they burn Anti-Papists and hang Papists" and said he would be of the King's religion or none at all.

Parliament enacted that all determinations concerning religion, faith and ceremonies adopted with the sanction of the King should be received, believed and practised, even if they were contrary to former injunctions, and the ceremonies of the consecration of bread and water and bearing ashes, palms and tapers for the Church services were revived, and in thirty-nine of the London parishes over two hundred persons were presented for the non-observance of these rites, for neglecting to have masses sung for the souls of their relations, for having sheltered Latimer, Barnes and Garret, for holding services in their houses, for having denied that the

Head of the Church was God himself, for having discussed the Scriptures and even for saying that they
preferred a sermon to a mass; but they were released
on promising Audley that they would appear before the
Star Chamber on All Hallows Day.

An unexpected change took place in course of time.

Henry had, on the death of the last Bourchier Earl of
Essex, given his title with some of his lands to Cromwell
and, on that of the Earl of Oxford, the high office of
Lord High Chamberlain. Attending the Privy Council
on June 10th (1540) he was accused of high treason by
the Duke of Norfolk, arrested and sent to the Tower.
The only man of position that sympathised with him was
Cranmer who saw in him the safety of the Reformation.

A bill of attainder was brought against him charging
him with setting at liberty some prisoners suspected of
treason; granting permission for the export of horses,
corn and other articles; having bestowed honours and
favours assuring the recipients that the King would
approve of it; giving permission for Englishmen and
foreigners to cross the seas without search and of having
made a large fortune, living in great state and failing
to give honour to the nobility. To these the Catholics
added that he had aspired to the hand of the Princess
Mary and had sought to obtain the church at Wells
of which he was dean. The Bill was passed and so ended
the life of the greatest man in England of his time.

A servant of the pomp-loving Wolsey, he differed from
his master in the simplicity and unostentatiousness of
his life, preferring the privilege of exercising power to
its outward show. The son of a blacksmith, he rose to
be Chancellor of the Exchequer, Knight of the Garter,
Vicar-General and Vice-Regent of the King, the creator
of the fleet, the organiser of the army and the second
man in the kingdom. He certainly did amass riches,
but he spent his money lavishly in the service of the

state and had at his command an army of spies in England and abroad for although, like all the Tudors, Henry was not wanting in personal courage, he had a terror of secret sedition, and every time Cromwell warned him of impending danger his influence was increased. His statesmanship raised him to supreme authority, and but few men could have coped with the troubles of the Dissolution. A follower of the teaching of Machiavelli, he struck at the noblest game, and among the victims of his policy were the high-minded Fisher and the abbots of Glastonbury, Reading, Whalley, Sawley, Woburn, Jervaulx and St. John's and the unflinching brothers among the Carthusians; among the nobles, the Poles, the Courtney's, the d'Arcy's, the Hussey's and the Percy's and among the scholars, Sir Thomas More. Catholic and Protestant alike fell under his judgment and Parliament, judges and juries were alike subservient to him. His cynicism and disregard of human life were apparent in the brevities of notes upon his papers such as "Item the Abbot of Reading to be sent down *tried and executed*"; "Item to know the King's pleasure touching Master More", and "Item when Master *Fisher shall go to his execution*". While Wolsey was hated by the nobility, he was supported by the clergy; but Cromwell was hated by both, and his only friends were among the Reformers; a friendship dangerous to him when he was in danger and, when he was "beknaved" by the King, he had no one to help him.

His last venture was an attempt to unite the Protestants of North and South Germany into an alliance against the Emperor who alone could have stemmed the Reformation. Had he succeeded in winning over Francis, Protestantism would have been strong enough to have prevented the Seven Years War, but the German princes shrank from an open rupture with the Emperor and when Francis, seeing that such an alliance would have boded ill for the Catholics of France, left Henry to bear the brunt of the strength of the Hapsburgs alone, he did not scruple to abandon his faithful servant to the fury of the reactionaries and Cromwell was beheaded in 1540.

Instead of erecting thirteen bishoprics the King contented himself with erecting six.

1. At the suppression of Oseney Abbey a new See was created and the abbey church was made the cathedral (1542); but, when Wolsey's foundation was surrendered to the King in 1545, the bishop's seat was transferred to St. Frydeswyde with a dean, eight canons, and one hundred students. This establishment is at once diocesan and collegiate, having a dean, six canons (of whom five are professors), the cathedral staff, students (in other colleges fellows) and undergraduates.

2. The abbey of Medehampstead had been burned down twice, being of remote antiquity as it was built originally to celebrate the conversion of Paeda about 656. The abbot possessed great privileges in the soke and till the nineteenth century his successor, the bishop, appointed the high bailiff, constable and other officers.

3. The church of Christ and the Virgin at Chester occupied the site of one of great antiquity originally dedicated to SS. Peter and Paul as the bishops of Mercia had a seat here till Peter Lichfield removed the See to St. John's. It was afterwards removed to Coventry in 1102 and we find the Bishop described as of Coventry and of Lichfield and "Chester."

4. The Augustinian house of Bristol was founded by Fitz Harding in 1142; only the gateway remains. Being made a cathedral in 1542, the See was united to that of Gloucester in 1836 and finally separated See in 1896.

5. The church of St. Peter at Gloucester was founded by Abbot Serlo between 1072 and 1104. On being made a cathedral in 1542 John Wakeman (Abbot of Tewkesbury) was made the first bishop.

6. The Abbot of Westminster (Benson) signed the deed of Dissolution and the complaisant abbot and monks were appointed dean and canons or were sent to the Universities with pensions of 3 marks to £10 each. The first and last bishop was Thirlby whose diocese included the county of Middlesex (with the exception of the Archiepiscopal manor of Fulham) with an income of £2,598 drawn from all parts of England but from this was to be deducted £40 a year for the Regius professors of Divinity, Law, Medicine, Greek and Hebrew, £116 13s. 4d. for the maintenance of twenty poor scholars at Oxford and Cambridge and a master and twenty scholars.

Although the penalties of the Six Articles had been abrogated and the death penalty was only inflicted after the third offence, Gardiner was so angered at the sympathy shown by Queen Katherine to the Reformers that he began to persecute them.

A priest, Pearson, who was noted for his eloquent attack on image worship; the singing man, Testwood, of Windsor Chapel, who had praised the attitude taken up by Luther, recommended the reading of the Bible and denounced image worship, and the churchwarden, Filmer, who had spoken scoffingly of the "fooleries of the priests" were arrested and condemned to the stake. The unfortunate (in more senses than one) Anne Askew was arrested and so severely racked that she had to be carried in a chair to Smithfield where, after refusing an offer made by Russel of a free pardon if she would recant, she was burned alive. Dean Harris (of Exeter), Sir Philip and Lady Holy (? Hobby), Sir John Clarendon and other members of the royal household were arrested and condemned to the flames through evidence taken at a previous trial which was (through the instrumentality of the Queen) found to be false and Gardiner's agents were indicted for perjury.

A notable case was that of Marbeck among whose writings were found written commentaries upon the Bible and the commencement of a Concordance of the Bible down to the letter M which Gardiner declared would, if published, destroy the use of Latin. Henry, who loved the Bible, declared that he could find no heresy in this, and he was pardoned.

The King then wrote a book entitled *The Necessary Doctrine and Erudition for any Christian Man*, in which he took a position midway between the Papal and Reformed Faiths, being rather inclined towards the latter; maintaining that the great principles of Justification was by the Grace and Mercy of God; modifying the question of the Worship of Saints and omitting the article on Purgatory, besides granting rights to National churches and encouraging the use of the Vernacular to meet the wants of the people.

Convocation, seeing that the people would not be content with the Vulgate and that they could not stem the growing desire for an Authorised Version of the Bible, proposed that the Bible should be again revised and intended to keep many Latin words such as Ecclesia, Poenitentia, Simulacrum, Episcopus, Confessio, Hostia, etc., but their endeavours came to nought as Henry (mistrustful of their intentions) was determined that the revision should be entrusted to the Universities.

In the following year, the free reading of the Bible was granted to the chancellor, officers of the army, magistrates, judges, the Speaker of the House of Commons and all persons of noble rank (male and female) by themselves or their servants in their own house, orchards and gardens and to all traders, heads of households in private but not to 'prentices and workpeople.

Bonner gave injunctions to his clergy to permit the laity to read the Bible or any other similar book after due prayer and preparation and ordered every priest in his diocese to read and study, one chapter of the New Testament every week from the first chapter of Matthew to the end of the Apocalypse and to instruct every child in his parish to read it in English. He also instructed them to live temperate lives, to avoid going to taverns or to play unlawful games, to perform their offices decently and to suffer no plays to take place in their churches, to explain the Gospels and Epistles and incite their people to do good works and to pray with them and explain the meaning of the ceremonies of the Church and to set forth the excellencies of virtue and the vileness of sin but to forbear reciting the fabulous legends.

Although, on his return from the North, Henry had held a public service of thanksgiving to God for having given him so excellent a wife as Catherine Howard, when he heard of her light conduct before marriage, he did not hesitate to order her to be removed to Sheen and, when certain of her friends had been tried by a jury for treason and hanged, she and Lady Rochford (sister-in-law of Anne Boleyn) were attainted and beheaded on Tower Hill.

There only remained of the Yorkist line the Countess of Salisbury and her younger sons and Edward Courtney. As the cardinal was out of his reach, Geoffry and Richard Pole were too weak to be considered dangerous and Courtney was in prison, he wrecked vengeance upon the aged Countess (1541) thus securing himself against any anti-dynastic plots. The only possible opponent was the Duke of Norfolk (descended from Thomas Duke of Gloucester, younger son of Edward III) but he bided his time for dealing with him.

By an Act of Parliament all parishes were compelled to set a copy of the Bible in the churches by All Hallow tide under pain of forty shillings for the delay of every month. The people were charged not to dispute it or to

Q

disturb Divine Service by reading it during Mass, but to read it humbly and reverently for instruction and edification and Bonner posted notices that none should read it in vainglory or draw persons together to listen to them.

Many sent their children to school to learn to read and others commenced to argue from certain passages, especially those relating to the Communion in both kinds and the use of an unknown tongue in the service which made Bonner threaten to remove the Bible if that continued.

About two years after the execution of Lady Catherine Howard, Henry thought of taking another wife and fixed Catherine Parr as the object of his choice. This lady claimed descent from Ivo de Taillebois and Lucy of Mercia through the female line and was fourth cousin to the King. The date of her birth is disputed, being generally given as 1510; but, from a correspondence concerning her proposed marriage with a son of Lord Dacre it would seem that she was under twelve in 1524. She married Lord Borough on whose death she married Lord Latymer whom she persuaded to stand aside during the rebellion of the Catholic nobles known as the Pilgrimage of Grace. Although by his will dated 1542 or 1543, he appears to have been a supporter of that Faith, as he left the rents and profits of the parsonage of Askham Richard and of the church of St. George in York to the master of the hospital and vicar of Wells for forty years to found a grammar school and to pray for him.

Being left a widow for the second time about the age of thirty with two large jointures, her hand was sought in marriage by the brother of Lord Hertford—Sir Thomas Seymour—but she preferred to take the risk of becoming queen consort, telling the King that it "were better to be his mistress than his wife". As she was closely connected with the King, Cranmer issued a special license authorising Henry to marry "Katherine de Latymer, wife of Lord Latymer, deceased in any church, chapel or

Oratory." The ceremony took place in the Queen's Closet in Hampton Court on July 12th, 1543, being celebrated by Gardiner (Bishop of Winchester) and witnessed by the Princesses Mary (to whom she gave a ruby bracelet and twenty pounds in money) and Elizabeth, the King's niece, Lady Mary Douglas, and the bride's sister, Mrs. Herbert (afterwards Countess of Pembroke), her friend Katherine Willoughby (Duchess of Suffolk) and Lady Jane Dudley, while the King was attended by Lords Hertford and Russel, Thomas Darcy, Edward Baynton, brother-in-law to the late queen, Sir Anthony Denny and William Herbert, brother-in-law to the bride, in the presence of a brilliant Court, and an obsequious Parliament passed yet another Act of Succession by which the crown was to devolve successively upon the children of Katherine and then upon Edward, Mary and Elizabeth and their heirs, with an ultimate limitation to the children of his sister the Duchess of Suffolk, the Scots line being passed over.

Charles V fell out with Paul III and Henry urged him to take the opportunity to assert the supremacy of the temporal power and to demand the holding of a free and separate council (as he did not acknowledge the summoning of that of Trent) to settle the questions that were disturbing Christendom. As Francis was protecting the Turkish interests in the East of Europe, they agreed to make war against him and as a first condition the Emperor demanded the declaration of the legitimacy of the marriage of his aunt (but was satisfied with the verbal assurance that Mary should come next to Edward in the succession) and that neither prince should make a peace until Henry was in possession of Ponthieu, Montreuil, Arras and Boulogne and Charles of the Duchy of Burgundy, Abbeville, Peronne, Hamme and St. Quintin. The Emperor invaded France by the Upper Rhine and advanced as far as the Marne and when Francis saw that

Paris was open to his attack he offered to make a separate peace which was supported by the promise of the emperor to be present at the Council of Trent and Henry was left to hold his own with the King. Having lost Boulogne, Francis endeavoured to retake it, having 40,000 mercenary troops from Italy; but, as they deserted in great numbers from day to day, the French King requested Paul to allow him a subsidy of 6,666 crowns instead of them. Peace was made by which Henry was to receive 100,000 crowns and an annuity of 10,000 crowns for eighty years, but, in 1550, Boulogne was returned to the French crown having cost England over £400,000.

During his absence in France he left Catherine as regent, and she spent much time in devotional exercises. She wrote *The Lamentations of a Sinner*, which is considered to be of equal literary value with the writings of Sir Thomas More, and had the Scriptures explained to her and her ladies (all of whom were more or less attached to the Reformation) by the learned Myles Coverdale and Nicholas Udall, who helped her in translating the Paraphrase of the Four Gospels. It was a notable sign that there were a great number of women (noble and simple) about the court at that time given to the study of devout sciences and strange tongues. It was a common thing to see young virgins so "nouzled" and trained in the study of letters that they willingly set all pastimes at nought for learning's sake and to see queens and ladies of most high estate and progeny embracing virtuous exercises, reading and writing, and, with most earnest study, early and late, applying themselves to the acquiring of knowledge instead of courtly dalliance. The Queen wrote "Thanks be given unto the Lord that thou has sent us such a Godly and learned King in these latter days to rule over us, that with virtue and force God's wise words have taken away the veils and mists of error and brought together in the Knowledge of the Truth of the light of

God's words. But our Moyses and most godly wise
governor the King hath delivered us out the hand of
Pharaoh. I meane by the Moyses King Henry the eight
my most favourite lord and husband." She also wrote
Prayers and Meditations, and a Latin epistle to the Lady
Mary urging her to let the translation of Erasmus'
Paraphrase of the New Testament be published in her
Highness's name.

Gardiner and Wroithesley were carefully watching to
find some opportunity to arouse the king's displeasure;
but, as they dared not accuse her publicly, they plotted
for the arrest of her sister Ladies Herbert, Jane Grey
and Tyrwhitt for breaches of the Six Articles.

In order to divert the King from his sufferings caused
by an ulcerated leg and to win him over to a further
stage in the Reformation, she would discuss matters of
doctrine with him; and, even in the presence of Gardiner,
remonstrated with him for withdrawing permission for
the circulation of a version of the Bible already authorised.
His answer was that it was not pleasant in his old age
(he was only fifty-four) to be taught by his wife and the
Bishop took advantage of this circumstance to obtain
an order for her arrest. On the following day he appeared
in the gardens of Whitehall with a strong guard, but the
King ordered them away with strong language and,
when Catherine pleaded for him, he told her that she
did know how he had "beknaved" her and his name
was struck out of the list of councillors.

The reform in the ritual of the Church was very slow.
As we have already seen there were diverse rites in the
Church: those of Sarum with its variants of Bangor and
Lincoln and Exeter; Hereford and York and, till 1414,
that of London. The services had become very compli-
cated and it was more difficult to find out the various
prayers than to repeat them and, consequently, the
clerks became careless and irreverent, as at Exeter the

choristers amused themselves with pouring wax from their candles on the heads of those below them and in some cathedrals the canons would calmly walk in at the beginning of a service, bow to the altar and walk out again. (*Everyman's History of the Prayer Book*, page 156.)

The spirit of Reform aimed at simplifying the services. Luther directed his energies to the removal of abuses but owing to the influence of the schoolmen he retained many Roman ceremonies. Calvin was opposed to all ceremonial, and turned his attention to Psalm singing and preaching.

In the eleventh century in England Osmund of Sarum tried to reconcile the Saxon and Norman Churches.

In the sixteenth century there was a feeling that some revision of Breviary was necessary and Cardinal Quinones and Hermann, Archbishop of Cologne, issued the "Reformed Roman Breviary" and the "Consultum," which last was largely used by Cranmer in revising the first Prayer Book. In 1534, William Marshal issued a "Prymer in English with certain prayers and godly meditations, very necessary for all people that understand not the Latin tongue." The Primers were not strictly speaking service books but contained certain portions of the services, the Penitential Psalms, the Litany and Private Prayers for special occasion, as well as graces before and after meat, the Catechism and even the alphabet. Another was issued under royal authority in 1537, and, in 1547, various experiments were made in respect to reforming the Church Services one of which was the publication of the "Rationale or explanation of the ceremonies in use in the Church of England", two drafts of the Services in Latin and the inclusion of the Litany translated by Cranmer from which in the time of Elizabeth (in spite of the recent recollection of Smithfield fires) the words praying for deliverance "From the tyranny of the bishop of Rome and detestable enormities" were

omitted. Henry lost his guide by the execution of
Cromwell and his mind was distracted by the fear of
civil war on his decease.

The country was divided into those who remained
as loyal to old state of affairs as was consistent with their
personal safety, and the events that occurred after the
Pilgrimage of Grace made them still more cautious,
and those who were in favour of reform. The first were
led by the Duke of Norfolk, the richest and the most
influential man in the realm after the King himself.
Descended in the female line from the Fitzalans, he had
married a daughter of the Duke of Buckingham descended
from Thomas of Brotherton, son of Edward III, and
before the birth of Prince Edward, had been looked upon
as a possible heir to the throne. The second party looked
to the Earl of Hertford who likewise claimed royal
descent by a marriage of one of his ancestors with a
lady of the family of March.

The Duke saw that his party was losing ground and
tried to unite his family with that of his opponent, by
marrying the highly gifted Lord Surrey to a daughter
of Lord Hertford and his daughter, the widowed
Duchess of Richmond (who was favourable to the Reformation) to Sir Thomas Seymour, but neither of his
children were agreeable and it was commonly said that
the Earl of Surrey refrained from marriage in order to
marry the Princess Mary.

Henry, seeing that in case of his death strife would
break out between the parties, and that his infant son
would be likely to be the bone of contention between
them, was determined to act vigorously to prevent it.
The introduction of trial by attainder made it easy to
dispose of powerful lords and, accordingly, Norfolk and
his son were suddenly arrested, the latter for having
quartered the arms of Edward the Confessor and
Thomas of Brotherton and the former for having, as

Earl Marshal, agreed to it and of having improperly revealed the secrets of the Council.

The Earl was tried by a grand jury at the Guildhall and executed on January, 1547. Although the Duke submitted to the King, stating the many services he had rendered the state and surrendering his estates to the King as an appanage to the Prince, the bill of attainder was passed in the Lords on January 27th and the day of his execution was fixed for the following day.

But on the night of January 27th (1547) the King was seized with his last attack and he died early next morning, a few hours before the time fixed for the execution; and as Edward VI refused to inaugurate his reign by a deed of bloodshed, the Duke was pardoned and his estates were restored; but he remained in the Tower for eight years, after which he returned to his seat at Kenninghall, a broken man.

In his last moments, Henry sent for Cranmer, the only man who survived the storm of the Dissolution. It is easy to criticise a man who lived during the stress of stormy times and to say that he fell short of his ideal. He has been blamed because he acted as a willow rather than an oak, but the second would have been torn up by the roots while the first bowed to the wind and in all his life he showed himself to be sincere and more than once saved the Reformation by yielding on minor points.

Thus ended the life of a great King who had been looked upon as the impersonification of Machiavelli's "Prince" and was an early example of the axiom "L'Etat, c'est moi". His works as a Church reformer in points of doctrine were negligible, but he paved the way for the drastic reforms of Somerset and Northumberland which had a temporary set-back under Mary and were established as the national Church by Elizabeth.

THE END OF THE SECOND PART

INDEX

INDEX

A

D

E

F

G